SECRETS of ARGYLL

By
Gerry Burke

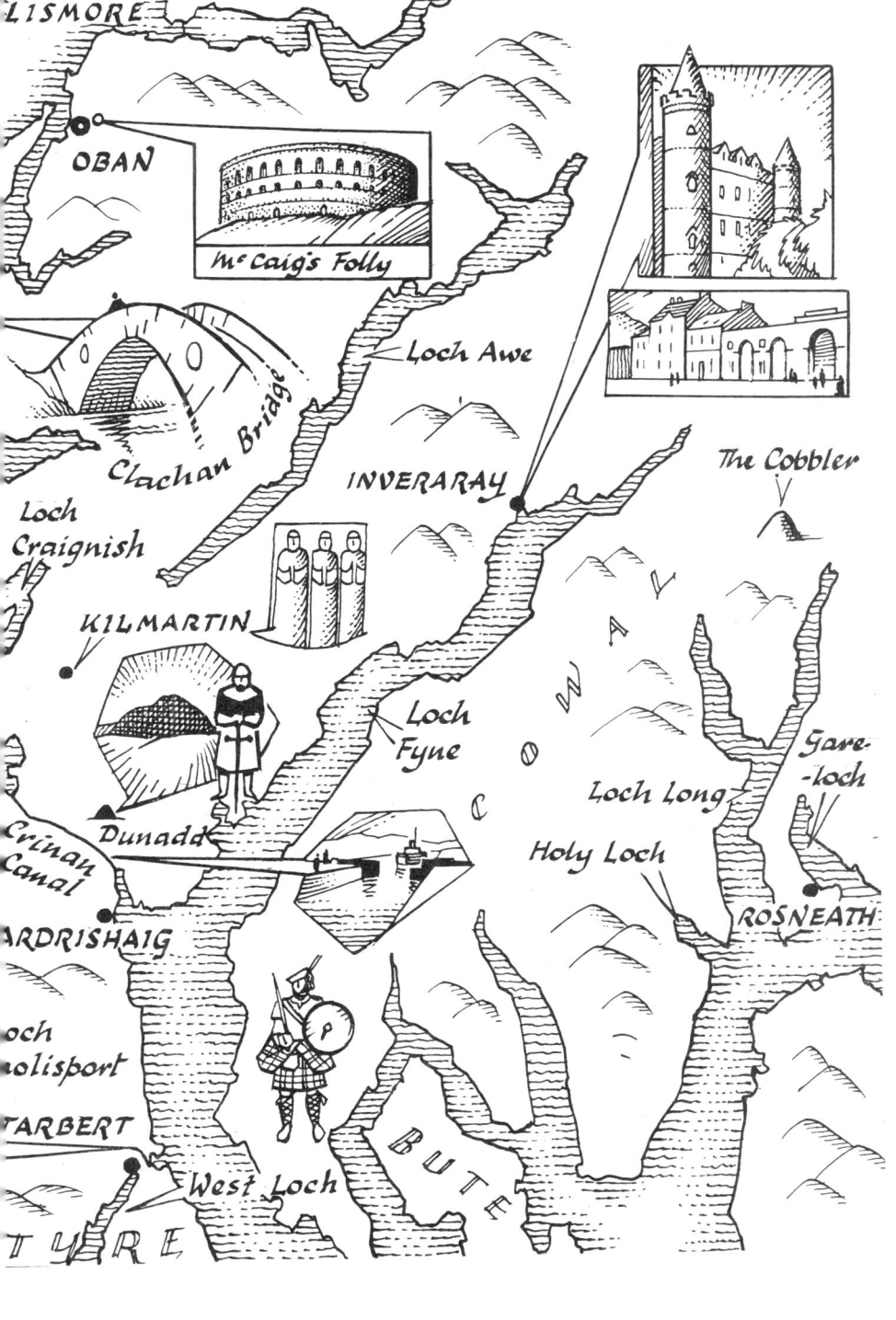

"Discover the Secrets and Splendour of Argyll" was published by Lang Syne Publishers Ltd, Old School, Blanefield, Glasgow G63 9HX in 1990 and printed by Waterside Printers.
COPYRIGHT LANGSYNE PUBLISHERS 1990.
Stories, other than those by Gerry Burke which are published here for the first time, were previously published in the Scots Magazine, with the exception of the chapter on Loch Awe which was previously published in The Highlander.
ISBN No. 185217 176.6.

Introduction

How did Government officers frame a man for murder in a desperate attempt to stop another Jacobite Rebellion? Where can you see a red London double decker bus crossing the Atlantic? What brought the boom times to Oban, a place that was little more than a cluster of thatched bothies until the mid 18th century? Why did a king have the heads of MacDonalds cut off and half boiled? Who put Inveraray on the world map after the hills and glens of Argyll burned themselves into his soul?

These are just some of the questions answered in "Discover the Secrets and Splendours of Argyll", a magical mystery tour of one of Scotland's most exciting and historic areas.

We explore Loch Awe where the grim ruined castles around its shores are silent reminders of the days when clan fought clan. The church with a phantom handprint, the piper executed for playing a wrong tune, and the silver coin of doom are just some of the tales featured here.

We investigate the ancient civilisations who had their homes in Argyll at the dawn of history and discover how, many centuries later, Viking invaders declared mainland Argyll an island after hauling boats overland.

You can also find out about: soldiers who faced a hangman's rope rather than a life as street beggars, the hydro power pioneers who died in dire straits, the secrets of the travelling folk, the grave cursed for eternity where nothing will grow except ugly dock leaves and nettles, murder and mayhem when the navy tried to press gang locals into service on the high seas, the 11th century holy cross emblazoned in the roof of a cave said to have been used by St Columba, the modern Robinson Crusoe who walked around without a stitch of clothing, the remarkable saga of Oban's unfinished colosseum, and many other well known and not so well known yarns of Argyll.

Calendars at the dawn of history

I am indebted to the following personalities for participating, albeit unwittingly, in the production of this brief encounter with the forces of darkness and blinding illumination, and shades in between, which helped to shape and expand the ancient pagan kingdom of Dalriada into the partially tamed wilderness that has survived as the Argyll of the present day.

These include: Walt Disney, St Columba, Fergus mor macErc, Robert Louis Stevenson, various druids (dead and alive), some tinkers, all of the dukes of Argyll, numerous barbarous caterans who hacked their own bloody chapters with the pitted edges of their claymores, some old Highland Hectors, the MacLeans and all the other Macs.

This slightly truncated odyssey of a few thousand years comes awake with the pre-druid sunrise, gets off its knees in the Holy Land, battles its way through a few European kingdoms, casts up on the sacred isle of Iona, clears up some popular misconceptions and throws new light on old mysteries to unlock some of the secrets of Argyll.

But back, far back, first of all to events which influenced such a small and sparsely populated kingdom to throw up not only so many bizarre and bloodthirsty dramas but also inspired a society structure that appears positively Utopian.

The standing stones of Argyll, like those at Stonehenge and Callanish, are hewn evidence of a strange civilisation that bewilders us to this day. They reflect an image of Druidical rites of blood sacrifice, beseeching the "God" sun and howling at the moon wherever they stand.

In the great plain of the flattest farming land around Killinochonoch, near Kilmartin, they are numerous, flanked by crypt-like burial chambers and other strangely inscribed rock faces. Singly and in clusters at dusk on the Moine Mhor they present an eerie prospect to the most un-fey traveller.

If any of these inanimate objects can pivot the focus of wonder and speculation, imagination, or whatever, to an age beyond record and mysterious purpose it is the single sentinel stone towering above Loch Craignish halfway above the Bealach on the hairpin bend of the road north of Kilmartin. It betrays the most sinister aspect of all and seems to cast a grave-stalking shadow in the face of the setting sun. Indeed it is reputed to mark the burial spot of a Viking prince.

The assumptions are that the precise positions of these stones and their shadows in relation to bearings of the sun were the basis of a highly developed equinoctial calendar system for a sophisticated agricultural ritual revolving around exact sowing and planting times and other events. Sacrifices, human and animal, are believed in certain eras to have been involved at complementary stone altars.

Given that the sun was the "God" to be humoured and appeased the Craignish stone could hardly occupy a more prominent sacrificial site. From a vantage point behind the monolith, perhaps where a long-vanished sight stone reputedly stood, the setting sun at a certain time of year slips exactly down through the V between the Paps of Jura to disappear into the Atlantic. Breathtaking is truly the only description for the panaromic vista from up here at dusk as the bronzed orb of the celestial deity gradually saps its glow from the scatter of paradise islands in the loch way below then reduces evey hump and bump on the glittering sea loch to a a series of dark velvet silhouettes. The occasional observer sees his own shadow vanish abruptly and feels compelled to remove his person equally quickly.

The entire vicinity of this Mid-Argyll area is a massive open-air museum of artefacts and natural wonders. In her splendid archaeological guide to this area published many years ago, Marion Campbell of Kilberry lists around 200 individual sites where the natives have left their mark possibly from as far back as 4,000 years before the birth of Christ, before the construction

Such is the density of the tangible traces left by following Bronze Age, Iron Age, Druidic and Pictish peoples that those uncovered so far are probably only surface scrapings. The thrust of a plough, the fall of a tree, change of course by a burn or drainage of a marsh is quite likely to unearth all manner of new finds. Indeed such is the regularity of accidental discoveries Miss Campbell makes an appeal in her booklet for any new ones to be brought immediately to the attention of the police, after first pinpointing the exact area with the minimum of disturbance. And the mention of reward for hidden treasure is not made lightly. Nor is the reminder about respect for other people's property.

As time goes by even previously discovered sites and objects can have new light thrown upon the very reason for their existence by continuing research into seemingly unrelated subjects.

It is worth diverging briefly to give an instance of a tantalising current example nowhere near exploited yet to its possible potential.

In the ancient graveyard at Kilmartin behind the truly picturesque church are medieval stones and a 9th century standing cross. The site is administered by the ancient monuments department of the Scottish Office and visited by thousands of folk evey year who, perhaps, saw nothing particularly remarkable about the very faded, in some cases undecipherable, etchings on the gravestones. The centuries have erased the earliest inscriptions and later names have been added. What is clear to see in some instances is a carved sword of Crusader appearance and a skull and crossbones.

The significance of this was lost on myself and everyone else until we read the findings of two authors who had already investigated the age old mysteries of the origins and concepts of Freemasonry and, additionally, their relationship or otherwise with that mysterious band of Chevaliers known from the days of the Crusades in the Holy Land as the Knights Templar.

Very briefly, these Knights of the Temple of Solomon were possibly the earliest form of international bankers, using a system of "travellers' cheques", arranging safe passage for pilgrims from all over Europe to the Holy Land in those days of piracy on the high seas; and plunder and murder on the horseback and camel sections. They were noblemen of the highest valour and integrity at the forefront of the battle to safeguard Christianity against the infidel. Back in their headquarters in France their wealth and military might was enormous and was eventually seen as a threat to the power of the Monarch. Charges of Satanism and other corruptions were drummed up against them and those that could be seized in a vast military purge met the most hideous deaths. Their leader, Jacques de Moulay, was spit roasted alive to exact a confession of his alleged crimes and the whereabouts of the Order's vast treasure.

It is known, however, that the lightning action was unable to prevent part of the Templars' fleet from sailing to safety with, apparently, their treasure ship. At sea they may have scattered but it was known that some arrived safely in Britain and certainly somewhere in Scotland where they lent their considerable fighting skills with horses to Robert the Bruce with tremendous effect.

These investigators were, centuries later, trying to trace their subsequent movements and settlements with varying degrees of success in different parts of Europe, when they heard a rumour that a Templar grave was thought to be on an island in a remote Argyll loch. There had never previously been any obvious indication of a Templar presence on the west of Scotland and they were thrilled at the possibility of a notable discovery.

The first chapter detailing their investigations and initial failure and some very mysterious recent burial activity are quite thrilling and certainly intriguing since they do not name the specific areas they searched, although I am pretty certain I have pinpointed them from the clues.

Their early disappointment, however, turned to bewilderment when they stopped off on their homeward journey at the Kilmartin Hotel for a meal and a casual look at the churchyard over the road. Their excitement knew no bounds when they found what they were looking for staring them in the face. Here was evidence of some kind of Templar settlement hidden through the centuries of history. Their failure, however, to come up with any further speculation was, to me, a disappointment.

Through local knowledge I can recall similar graves in the area and can only wonder at the moment if certain long-established pedigrees in Mid-Argyll are in fact descended from such Holy Land pioneers. There were very good reasons for keeping their presence secret and the potential implications are enticing. Did their treasure ship tie up in Crinan, for example, or did it in fact come out of hiding only in recent times to finance a "project" elsewhere still shrouded in mystery and international speculation? At least the skull and crossbones they flew from the masts of their ships has lost a little of its mystery on a simple grave in an old Argyll churchyard.

The crucial point is that here in this corner of the realm is an overflowing font of living history with coded messages all around waiting to be read with international interest.

On the fantasy side more than one best seller or movie with a supernatural or sci-fi theme has been inspired by the inexplicable fragments and indentations left by those people who remain in the shadows of time.

Whose are the footprints in ancient stone that leave a trail from Ireland through Kintyre, in south Argyll, on Dunadd, and out to the farthest Hebrides? Certainly in human form they are occasionally accompanied by those of a dog or a cat. Local tradition sometimes describes the clearly identifiable foot prints as those of Columba. On Dunadd, alongside indecipherable Ogam script and a sculpted Pictish carving of a wild boar, there is a theory that one of the footprints was used in a rather clever Coronation rite which ensured fealty to the ancient High Kings by their minion potentates in a Celtic realm which could have stretched from Cornwall to Cape Wrath.

Rather than have the King set his foot physically on the territorial earth of his fiefdoms, involving massive arduous journeys, would perhaps a token handful of the very soil be brought from the farthest reaches of his kingdom, so that he might stamp his authority without venturing from his fortress?

Royalty in Britain today is passed down with rituals not so far removed.

We fumble in the dark at this stage of history, before Columba arrived with his timeless message of Christianity.

And, seriously, does Arthur of the Round Table figure in this conundrum?

The ages of his alleged presence and the whereabouts of his Avalon are as vague as the reflection of a candle on the wall of a darkened cave.

Glastonbury may indeed be the popular shrine for devotees of the Arthurian legends, but his battles took him at least as far as the natural fortress of what is now Dumbarton Castle. Stand on the summit on anything but a foggy day and the eye travels right up the length of the Holy Loch, still a safe anchorage in Argyll for warships — and the territory of the ancient Clan MacArthur, mac being the Gaelic for son of. Ben Arthur, or the Cobbler mountain, which straddles the Argyll-Dunbarton border rears at the head of adjacent Loch Long.

Now, if an eminent American expert on the subject can seriously suggest that Arthur's genuine round table lies under centuries of slag heaps by the old ironworks of the Carron River near Falkirk, and that the base of Arthur's O'On certainly lies in a nearby council house garden, why shouldn't we examine the suggestion that the elusive figure left his progeny to proliferate on the Cowal peninsula of Argyll?

Documentation on the certain existence of the shrine-like O'On does exist, by the way, and even in those days the distance is nothing and the possibility of a strong presence in that part of Argyll entirely logical.

Tradition has it that Clan Arthur was THE senior clan in Argyll long before the Campbells and even MacAlpine.

In his notes to the Dewar Manuscripts, a rare collection of transcriptions of oral history and folk tales on Argyll, funded by the Eighth Duke of Argyll in the mid 19th century, and edited by the distinguished Celtic scholar, Rev John MacKechnie, the Arthur connection is examined along with suggestions that both Campbell and MacArthur are descended from Clan Diarmid in Ireland, but that Arthur in its own right is referred to in early Irish and Welsh writings with reference to his sword *Caladbolg,* an old Irish Gaelic term later adapted to Excalibur or *Claidheamh Soluis* — the lightning sword. The notes go on at length with dizzying interwefts and twists and turns and references to the symbols at Dunadd, including the Boar's Head carving, which appears in the Campbell chief's coat of arms.

A song quoted at the start of the manuscripts has the line :—
"Hills, ills and MacAlpines, but when did MacArthur come." Perhaps if we knew the rest of the words we could solve the whole heritage mystery once and for all and probably close down an international intrigue that has defied historians through the ages.

St Columba and the Iona missionaries

Iona — 563. St Columba, missionary priest of the warrior family of the High King of Ireland set foot this year on Scottish soil, and helped change the course of history in the British Isles.

This part of Argyll at this time was known as Dalriada, claimed earlier from the Picts by a tribe of Irish known as the Scotti, the sons of Fergus mac Erc, king of the original Dalriada in Ulster.

Their headquarters was the ready-made fortress on Dunadd, surrounded by centuries of inherited culture and customs which were partly absorbed into their own form of lapsed Celtic Christianity.

When their countryman Columba arrived in the realm with his followers it was to Dunadd that he went, seeking approval for his mission, and a base from which to operate. It is likely the ruler was persuaded to offer at least grudging assistance, having heard tales of Columba's exploits in his native Ireland, where it was believed his monk's habit had been cast aside for the mantle of strategic battle adviser against what he regarded as the forces of evil, embodied in the high-King and his druidical advisers, threatening the overturn of Christianity. Thousands were slain in a quasi-religious rout but the taste of victory in God's name for Columba was apparently soured by his anguish over the huge loss of life. He was also at odds with other peers of the Celtic church over his perception of his duties, and it was then he decided to take his preachings elsewhere and to convert or reclaim as many souls as he felt he had been responsible for sending early to their maker.

He seems to have been a formidable man of unshakable faith, physical courage and total determination and self confidence, and could not have succeeded with less to even attempt the enormous challenge of instilling Christian worship and the mark of the Cross on the hearts of barbarous pagans who still believed in spells and charms and the blood and gore of ritual sacrifice.

From his base on Iona, he sent his brother monks out in all directions at considerable personal risk, to badger and cajole feared tribal chieftains all over Scotland into at least listening to their skilful entreaties on behalf of their "chief" and his all-powerful God.

Columba was regularly out on the campaign trail himself and there are countless legends concerning his art as diplomat, peacemaker and even maker of miracles.

He would stress, however, it was the hand of God that calmed the roaring whirlpool depths of the Corryvreckan, and saved his galley and crew from inescapable death by drowning — a fate suffered by countless wayward seafarers over the centuries.

And when he ordered the Loch Ness Monster to retreat to its lair and prey no more on hapless travellers, the well-recorded escapade would have gone down well with potential converts in old Inverness.

By the time of his death in 597 Columba's mark was to be found the length and breadth of Scotland. Churches and tiny cells and religious communities were established by his fellow preachers and those who came after them. The map of Scotland today gives an indication of their spread by the use of place names prefixed by Kil *(Cille: a church or cell)* as in Kilmartin, Kilninver, Kilpatrick etc.

Vikings claim new territory in Argyll

Later developments in history almost obliterated Columba's font of Christianity when the Vikings came in their turn to lay claim to new territory in Argyll and the west coast islands. Around the beginning of the ninth century marauding and systematic looting of Iona became so unendurable the religious order finally retreated back to Ireland before they too were wiped out. The illustrious Book of Kells went with them.

The longships were the scourge of the entire coastline and even beyond it in the most ingenious fashion. Tarbert on Loch Fyne gets its name from an old Norse word meaning a link between two sea lochs. There certainly isn't a waterway but that did not prevent one wily galley master using the wind in his sails to help power his vessel overland on rollers from the West Loch to Loch Fyne a mile away. The architect of this feat was Magnus, King of Norway, and having completed the manoeuvre he declared the peninsula of Kintyre must therefore be regarded as an island and, consequently, an official state of Norway.

The stunt was pulled in other areas which now share a similar name, and Robert the Bruce carried it out at the same place with similar good effect, on one of his later escapades, to save the potentially treacherous and arduous passage round the Mull of Kintyre. Nowadays the Crinan Canal which starts at Ardrishag up the road is the easy way out for vessels bound from the Firth of Clyde sea lochs for the west coast and the Atlantic beyond.

Over the years and after fresh campaigns more and more Viking and native blood that had not been spilt from the end of an axe became intermingled as the new invaders settled like homesteaders and founded their own clans with their familiar names, which now take up pages of the local telephone directory.

The final defeat for the Norsemen, however, came in 1263 at the Battle of Largs in the Firth of Clyde when their claims for the Lordship of the Isles were finally snuffed out.

History from here on is more the time of the clans with Argyll truly the wild west of tribal strife and struggle for supremacy.

For a focus on the clan system it might be as well to look initially on the Campbells — not because of their ancient lineage which is well and truly surpassed by those such as MacDonalds, MacLeans, MacLachlans, MacCallums etc., but because in spite of their comparatively late development they became the most powerful family in Argyll and one of the most feared and influential in Scotland, and even in England, Holland and France. They stood at the side of the throne in those countries but had sworn blood enemies among the lowest cottars in their own kingdom.

Few ancestral families have aroused as much controversy as Clan Campbell, whose present chief lives with his family at Inveraray Castle, on the banks of Loch Fyne.

The family whose history can be positively traced back to the time of Robert the Bruce have been forever tagged with the stigma of the Massacre of Glencoe which is enough for starters, and extensively recorded in other publications. But their inherent business acumen and gift for land and power broking, far execeeding the cruder plots and ploys of their neighbours, brought them their share of jealous enmity anyway. The saying, "Never trust a Campbell" lasts to this very day in some quarters and has been long-uttered on the west coast of Scotland by such as those mentioned above and by other clans like MacGregors, MacGillivrays, MacDougalls, Stewarts and so on. They seem to blithely forget that in those times few of them trusted the others with a handshake at a wedding. Where the house of Argyll was deft in the extreme with a quill pen and a property parchment these others left their signatures with the dextrous stroke of a weapon or a well-aimed firebrand.

Butchers, massacre and boiled heads

Around the middle of the last century, well within the scope of first hand and handed-down recall, George the Eighth Duke of Argyll decided to commission the largest collection of folk tales ever gathered in Scotland.

John Dewar, a Gaelic-speaking estate employee who worked in the forestry at Rosneath on the Gareloch, was seconded to travel the length and breadth of the western Highlands and islands with his copperplate pen and notepad to take down, virtually verbatim, a word picture of the lives and times of the clansmen whatever their badge or battle cry.

Dewar, "a precise, accurate old man, with a wonderful memory and small imagination", was briefed in the following terms: .... "I don't want you to drop a curtain on the murders and other misdeeds of the clan. On the contrary I want them written as they are told and the more the better, but as some few get praise from MacAuley there must be some good recorded of somebody in Argyll, and I have seen none of it recorded so far in the history of John Dewar. Don't let us make ourselves out to be worse savages than we are, but let us tell the truth and shame the de'il .... do people only remember Inverlochy and Glencoe and Allan Breac? Go ahead, Dewar."

The redoubtable Dewar thereafter piled his words high — over three quarters of a million of them in immaculate Gaelic on pages that were in themselves works of art — and posted off his dispatches wherever he came across a mail coaching post in the remotest corner of the county.

Bearing in mind the enormous transport problems of those days his feat was incredible, and the collection a delight for anyone with the remotest curiosity or concern for stirring Scots history and heritage. More the pity that so very few have even heard of his work, which was presented in a very matter-of-fact style as the following extracts show.

The Stewarts of Appin v The MacDonalds of Glencoe.
(Not the infamous Massacre)

"The MacDonalds of Glencoe", states Dewar, "were wont to carry off spoils (sheep, cattle, whatever) and some would be putting complaints against them to the King. One time, the laird of Fasnacloich (of the Stewarts of Appin) attended by a ghillie was passing through Glencoe. Some of the Glencoe men met them. They killed the laird of Fasnacloich .... The MacDonalds of Glencoe had done something that was bad against Maclain Stewart of Appin (the chief) who now sent a complaint against them to the king. The king sent a messenger to Maclain Stewart with orders to go to Glencoe to kill the Macdonalds and to fill Glencoe with stones but, nevertheless, he made the laird of Ardshiel, headman of the men of Appin, to go to Glencoe to kill all the Glencoe Macdonalds."

The tale, culminating in a horrific presentation to the king, continues in such pedantic matter-of-fact reportage perhaps because Dewar had recorded so many similar tales where only the names of clans and individuals had altered around the butcher's block

This comparatively minor squabble, however, appears to soften a little when the MacDonalds after successful flight into the hills turn the tables and finally have the unsuspecting laird of Ardshiel in the sights of a musket. Rare compassion intrudes, however. The son of the MacDonald refuses to pull the trigger because Ardshiel is dandling a toddler on his knee allowing him to play with the silver buttons on his greatcoat.

Eventually, however, as the original pursuers make their way homeward the MacDonalds spring an ambush of immensely cunning conception and are on the point of drawing buckets of helpless blood when a party of Camerons appear unexpectedly on the scene.

Possibly after tossing a coin, or perhaps cold-bloodedly weighing up the odds of keeping in favour with their closer neighbours, the Stewarts, they decide to throw in their hardware against the MacDonalds.

Cutting a long story short, the MacDonalds got their heads chopped off on the stump of a tree. The heads of MacDonald of Invercoe and his brother of Achatriochadain werre washed in a well still known today as *"Tobar nan Ceann"* (Well of the Heads. There are several others with similar grisly histories). The heads were then half-boiled to help preserve them and a local halfwit was sent to deliver them to the agents of the king in Perth. Dewar mentions that the king decided to outlaw the Macdonalds after this as just another matter of fact.

The Burning of MacDonald of Keppoch's House.

(Recorded verbatim from Archibald MacLean of Glaic then aged 85)

"My father was in the army in Prince Charles's year. It was under the command of the Duke of Argyll he was. He was at Culloden and he was at the burning of the house of MacDonald of Keppoch.

"It was a handsome house. It was a house of two storeys in height. The walls were white with lime and it was thatched with bracken. They set fire to it. MacDonald's lady went and sat on a hill near the house and looked at the soldiers burning it. When the house was burnt the soldiers gathered all the wooden dishes and vessels that were in the washing house with everything else in it that could be burnt and they burned them as well as the house itself and they left nothing of the lady's property that could be destroyed that they did not destroy.

"The poor Highlanders (presumably the Campbell/MacLean contingent of the Crown forces) durst not put a finger on any of the plunder. All that was given to the English. The English were sent at first to carry off the cattle and to plunder the houses and to carry off everything that was worth with them and then the Highlanders were sent to burn the houses and spoil the country.

"Those clans that joined the Prince thought that the Duke of Argyll's soldiers were worse than the English. But the Highlanders (Campbells) were obliged to obey orders and although they were spoiling with their hands their hearts were sorry that they were obliged to do it."

Clan Nail (The day it wiped itself out)

There is not, as far as the current telephone directory is concerned, any person of the surname Nail or MacNail living in the western Highlands. Yet they were supposed to have been a sizable tribe inhabiting Strath Eck in Cowal. They kept very much to themsleves and lived in perfect harmony until one of the local witches put the evil eye on them as they happily fished for salmon in the River Eachaig.

According to a local forester of the neighbouring MacIlvain tribe, one minute they were splashing about in the river, about 100 of them; the next they were wading in each other's blood.

The story told to Dewar was that the wife of an elder brother of the clan accused his younger brother of making a pass at her. Claymore drawn he went for the younger who simply acted in defence not knowing the reason for the attack. Others rushing to prevent an affray were too late to save the younger and the older was killed in the general tussle which developed due to a total misunderstanding over who had done what to whom. Since all were armed as a matter of course in those days there was virtually only a handful of unscathed survivors who left the district. The remaining widows married into the MacIlvains who as a result added another chunk of territory on to their own boundaries.

Why Duke told Queen: 'My men must hang!'

This is a tale about the Duke of Argyll as a general in the British Army in the war in Holland against France in which his men acquitted themselves with such valour that the Queen invited him to bring his army to London for a royal inspection.

She was puzzled when the Duke ordered three sets of gallows to be erected opposite the palace and Dewar's story, probably from MacLean of Glaic, who may have got it from a returned soldier called Grey Lachlan, quotes the Duke's explanation:

"Many of the soldiers who have fought in Holland have been wounded and some are old. They cannot work. They must not steal. And they would feel ashamed to go begging through the kingdom. It would be disgusting to myself to see them going as wretched tramps through the country in bad clothes and shoes asking food from those who might be willing to give it; and I think as we have got out of them all the work which they are able to do and that we need them not any longer the best thing we can do for them is to hang them and put them out of pain so that they may not grieve us, looking at them as poor, miserable creatures in bad plight."

The Queen said: "The soldiers must be looked to and something must be done for them. An Act of Parliament must be passed and an allowance must be granted them so that they shall not be dependent on their relations or on the country." Which. says Dewar, was done at the next sitting of Parliament so instituting British military pensions.

Now while this latter humorous tale has a certain ring of familiarity about the Highlander's breezy attitude to life and limb there can be no doubt from the rest of the stories, and from standard historical texts, that "letters of fire and sword" were a common form of intercourse in those days whether issued "legal y" by the Crown or otherwise.

Perhaps George Douglas, the Eighth Duke, did feel that for once the notorious Massacre of Glencoe might be reviewed against a fuller perspective of those bitter feuding times which is why he sent Dewar out into the field. Who knows?

The hydro pioneers who died for nothing

Glencoe is best known for the bloody massacre of the MacDonalds by the Campbells, but in the last years of the 19th century and the early years of the present one, many men and boys died in horrific circumstances. They were the workers who earned a handful of coppers a day in the savage struggle against the elements and crude machinery to harness the power of hydro-electricity.

Visitors pour through the glen each year in their thousands and crane their necks in justifiable awe at the majesty of the soaring mountains. More adventurous walkers of the West Highland Way can look down the Devil's Staircase and feel a justified sense of achievement on having made it to the top of the zig-zag track from the modern highway below.

But where is the plaque to the memory of the rag-tag army of thousands of navvies who scaled the heights in tattered coats and odd shoes, through blinding blizzards, to reach the site of the Blackwater Dam constructed by the British Aluminium and Light Company? Who recalls armed guards and a gunboat being called in to quell the strikes?

There is a pitiful little cemetery up there today near the scant remains of the massive wooden camp which testifies only a little to the harrowing cost to humanity of furthering the bounds of civilisation.

The pre-cast concrete grave stones simply give a name and a date with the inscription "Died at the Dam". They represent only a portion of the death toll.

On the site, in the foulest weather, men drowned in channels of mud, were crushed to death by steam-driven machinery and runaway rail bogeys. Many lost arms, legs or both when the explosives went off prematurely.

But dozens of others died just trying to get there for the supreme reward of the hardest physical work imaginable — sixpence in old money for each cubic yard of rock hewn out of the mountain side by pinch bar and sledge hammer.

The workforce came from all over Britain and from Ireland on foot, and few went back to their families with a penny even after two or three years at a stretch.

The death toll amongst those who succumbed on the mountain travel stages will never be known. Skeletons are uncovered periodically still but others remain pretty well preserved at the bottom of peat bogs they blundered into masked by a deceptive covering of snow.

In the bitterly cold midwinter of 1903 a Derbyshire father and son set out on the long tramp to Scotland. They had just two shillings (10 pence) between them and the boy, aged about 15, was leaving his mother for the first time.

The lad was in bad shape by the time they reached Bridge of Orchy and his father doubted whether they should continue. They were so close to the foot of the Staircase but the mountain, the final, treacherous stage, worried him severely. The boy insisted they go on.

They made it to the top. The father, half carrying his son, reached the summit and staggered blindly on to within hearing distance of the machinery.

He dragged himself and the boy on until he could be heard shouting for help. The men downed tools and raced to help, wrapping the youngster in the coats and jackets from their backs.

They rushed him to the heat of the steam from a powered hammer machine and tried to force hot liquid down his throat. But the boy was dead and it appeared his father had already been carrying a corpse. The grief stricken father gave his tearful evidence to a Fatal Accident Inquiry in Oban and went home to Derbyshire leaving his son in a crude grave at the "great works".

There are numerous other dreadful tragedies in old files and recorded in letters to newspapers at the time by some of the more eloquent navvies on the isolated site. The letters were anonymous for fear of retribution by the employers, but I would bet, having examined them, that several were written by Patrick McGill, the militant navvy turned author, who used his personal experiences up there as the basis of his book of the time: "Children of the Dead End".

There is only one woman's grave and the story connected with her demise is quite astonishing and appears to have some factual basis. She was a cook for one of the huts and a drunken navvy objected to her culinary standards by throwing her into her own fire and roasting her alive. Whether he ever saw the dock of a court is anyone's guess as the internal working of the camp was virtually a law unto itself.

Strong drink was behind much of the self-wrought carnage, there being no other pastimes beyond gambling and feud-fighting to pass away the hours between exhausted sleep and shift calls.

Many of those who died on the mountain met their end on their way home from the nearest pub — the King's House Hotel on the other side off the Glencoe Road. When the last penny was spent at the bar they carried their dulled wits and hangovers into the final whiteout.

Others cooked their own brew in the hills from potatoes and other vegetables and sold the rotgut round the camp in a constant battle of wits against armed companymen with orders to smash the stills.

Those bravados who sickened of the physical toil took to hijacking supplies wagons in Dick Turpin-type teams, frequently battling over the right to ambush a prize while the targeted coach and horses jogged past, the driver totally oblivious to the reason for the be-cudgelled mayhem. The clever ones simply waited until the great barrels of booze that came in by boat were landed on the pier at what is now Kinlochleven, and drilled through them from below while the stevedores above passed them off as returned empties.

On the day of the official opening, down in Kinlochleven, with five star facilities for the titled guests, the management in an uncharacteristic gesture decided to lay on a "drink facility" for the wild men down from the mountain who had actually done all the work. They took the precaution of calling in police reinforcements and erected a small timber caboose-type gaol to house any miscreants. And there were.

The inevitable riot broke out and a particular hammer-hard giant was pounced on by an army of constables. They succeeded in cuffing his hands behind his back, manacling his ankles together and joining the two with a length of chain before installing him in the caboose.

Trussed like a turkey, however, he managed to use his head to batter down a wall and was last seen bounding off like a wallaby into the hills. Only a few years ago there were men still living who could tell you they were there and their recall was quite impeccable!

Secrets of the travelling folk

Another aspect of Argyll which is seldom touched upon, is that indigenous "clan" which recognises no feudal lands.

The tinkers or travellers, but never in this area referred to as gypsies, have been pitching their "gellies" since the time of the Druids and possibly before. The earliest may well have been "gypsies" since they are likely to have been the original workers of metal who brought the bronze and iron ages from the far east.

They are a hardy, canny, and, perhaps essentially, by nature a rather secretive race away from their own. They have been and still are despised by some sections of the community. Others have a high regard for their traditional skills in crafting and agricultural work which are certainly dying out in line with just about every other type of manual skill. But they are a proud people within their own caste and have maintained their culture in the face of a world rapidly changing all around them. Those guardians of their folklore and customs like Belle Robertson and Duncan Williamson are probably now witnessing the greatest ever changes their people have faced.

Many of the travellers in Argyll will tell you they are descended from "the most noble clan in Scotland", the Stewarts. They also come commonly by the names of Cameron, MacDonald, Johnstone and MacPhee among others, and their ancestral history would be similar. They have never had any great regard for the Authorities and, perhaps, in less-enlightened days with some justification when they were always waiting to be moved on.

Their dialect, known as the cant, with Gaelic, English and other "gadge" nuances renders them less likely to be understood by even settled natives of the district they have commonly shared for generations.

They are certainly a lively race and unlike many other septs or sects in society tend to keep their excesses to themselves. This will sound patronising. Over the years I have had dealings with many and never had trouble with any. Quite the reverse.

Good luck to those who are now freely moving into a world of mod-con housing. There are those who are delighted with purpose-built sites for their caravans, now provided by law. But the landscape around Loch Fyne and other shores will be missing something when the last of the old willow-framed canvas gellies is gone.

Modern society, however, has assured their space is taken up by a replacement breed of nomads who puzzled Sheriff David Noble at the court in Oban in 1989.

He was dealing with an assault case in which two accused gave their address as the Raspberry Lay-by in Appin, and asked if they were travellers, hippies or tinkers. "New Age Travellers", they replied, thereby only partly satisfying the curiosity of those confounded by the sudden emergence of encampments of large numbers of "incomers", particularly of English suburban origins, including many with cultured accents and possibly old school ties holding their hair bunches in place.

At the time of writing the phenomenon is indeed most notable at the Raspberry Lay-by. A large garishly coloured wagon train of broken down buses, caravans and assorted trailers is pitched on the traditional tinker site on the road near Appin.

Oban's Colosseum and spa that never were

It is a curious fact that Oban, arguably the most important town in Argyll, has little in the way of historical heritage beyond the mid-nineteenth century.

The tracks and footpaths of earlier people seem to have passed by to the north and to the south although there have been recent discoveries of occupations by cave dwellers in neolithic times.

It is a sad sign of modern society that some of the caves in the area are occasionally occupied by members of the ever-increasing ranks of the homeless. Some were occupied after both wars by ex-servicemen who simply could not adjust to living under a conventional roof after years of warfare in the trenches.

Oban itself has become a mecca for visitors. Its obvious scenic attractions were first capitalised on in more gracious Victorian times.

The railway journey from Glasgow possibly ranks as the most sensational in Britain but, unfortunately, the splendid old station building and clock tower which served as the link between train and island car ferry have been demolished to make way for the soulless "lego-style" terminus that exists today.

Prince Charles's parents-in-law were among thousands who campaigned for retention and repair of the famous old structure but their voices were lost in the din of demolition.

Oban's most striking feature remains however, drawing awe and admiration from the countless thousands who come to visit year after year.

Sitting high above the town it is a magnificent granite-built rotunda which serves no practical purpose whatever beyond a focal and vantage point for inspired photographers.

This near replica of the Colosseum in Rome was the vision of beneficent Oban banker John Stuart McCaig who paid for its construction to provide work for the unemployed in the area in 1897.

The superb workmanship was not completed unfortunately. McCaig had intended a dome and 100 foot tower to complete the structure but the funds dried up and the building remains a thoughtfully preserved monument to his memory.

Over the years various enterprising and imaginative schemes have been floated to further capitalise on its dominant presence.

The most ambitious involved the provision of a cable car or chair lift from the north pier harbour area which, perhaps, deserved better consideration at the time.

Hidden away on a neighbouring eminence are the remains of another ambitious project which ran out of steam and money. The ruins of the huge Hydropathic spa hotel are now occupied only by the dainty roe deer herd when winter squalls and gales batter in from the Atlantic. The bucks and does appear oblivious to the incessant clamour of the traffic in the crowded streets below.

Other forms of wildlife seem to have adapted remarkably well to the imposition of a human settlement on their traditional domain and even thrive on the attention they receive.

Seals in the bay appear to positively relish performing uninhibitedly for the visitors' delight at extremely close quarters, and certain individuals even control their presence by feeding them fish scraps at certain times of the day.

The presence of the fishing fleet, or what remains of it, is an added incentive for them to maintain such a close relationship. The boats have dwindled in number and now the catches are mainly shellfish which are largely despatched direct to the Continent in convoys of massive container lorries.

The car ferries to the islands with their freight of building materials, foodstuffs and livestock, and the island pleasure boats, ensure a busy waterfront scene.

Progress has brought a better standard of visitor accommodation to the town but, unfortunately, the character of many of the watering holes remains unchanged and the essence of the area is stamped on more than a few.

The town itself was little more than a clutter of thatched bothies until the mid-18th century and the boom times only came with the railway line in 1880.

Expansion seems inevitable since not only are more and more visitors discovering the delights of this part of Argyll but ever-increasing numbers are actually selling up elsewhere and moving in for good, creating enormous pressures on the housing market and ancillary services.

Planners and developers have frequently cast an appraising eye across the narrow sound to the undeveloped island of Kerrera and several schemes involving the provision of a causeway have been promoted over the years.

The most recent involved a packed public meeting of townspeople and islanders with varying and hotly disputed views on the subject. The feasibility study remains on paper only so far but it will undoubtedly surface again when the protest element has been sufficiently softened up.

The original seat of power in this immediate area is more or less on the outskirts of the town at Dunstaffnage Castle, ancient seat of the MacDougalls, descended from the Norse-Celtic lords of the isles. The Stone of Destiny was lodged in their keeping here before being passed on into the custody of the monks at Scone.

Clan Campbell eventually took control of the castle and only recently beat off an "impertinent" takeover bid by a wealthy American industrialist who engaged lawyers to prove an ownership claim going back to the days of the earliest MacAlpine chiefs. The present Duke left him with a flea in his ear and a strong impression of the traditional Campbell facility and acumen in matters relating to property.

South of Oban is another magnet for the tourists and day-trippers from the town itself — the Atlantic Bridge; the splendid hump-backed structure designed by Telford in 1790, linking the island of Seil with the mainland, and still in use to this day as the only means of vehicle and pedestrian access. It is an astonishing spectacle to witness an ex-London Transport double decker bus negotiating the blind summit of the bridge which truly does cross the Atlantic over the Clachan Sound where the ocean tides are constrained in the breadth of a modest riverway.

Here on the island side is the Tigh an Truaish Hotel, the "house of the trousers", which got its unique title from the anti-Jacobite legislation imposed after the 1745 rebellion, banning the wearing of the kilt. Only soldiers in the service of the Crown were allowed to wear the national dress and on leave they had to change at this point into breeches or trousers.

At the other end of the island is the quaint village of Ellenbeich, a former slate miners' community of nearly 1,000, which with the island of Easdale across the narrow sound was virtually devastated after flooding by a freak storm during the last century.

Off to the north west across the sea from here is the island of Insh, just a mile long and famous for the Robinson Crusoe figure who inhabited its cave for months at a time in the summer after being made redundant in a Midlands factory.

He bought his dream island and wandered around starkers, a spirit freed from the grinding pressures of the twentieth century with only a passing yacht or fishing boat to cast a blur on his blue horizons.

Quite likely the same cave had provided similar shelter for one of Columba's followers who sought solitude and peace to commune with his maker in similar fashion.

Inveraray and Loch Fyne from the Bell tower.

Oban. Eventide reflections in the harbour waters.

The Kyles of Bute.

Campbeltown from across the loch.

Kilchurn Castle, Loch Awe.

Holy Loch.

By the shores of Loch Eck.

West Bay Dunoon.

The Holy Loch from Ardnadam Point.

Loch Leven and the Pap of Glen Coe.

The "Isle of Mull" approaching Oban Harbour.

Campbeltown Harbour, Kintyre.

Inveraray Castle.

Ardrishaig, Crinan Canal Basin.

Easdale Village on the Isle of Seil.

Loch Striven.

A bird's eye view of Inveraray and Loch Fyne.

Tarbert and Loch Fyne, Kintyre.

The Buachaille Etive Mhor, Glen Coe.

By the shores of Loch Awe.

Strone Gardens, Cairndow.

Sunset over Connel Bridge.

At Carradale, Kintyre.

Oban. McCaig's Tower.

The uninhabited Garvellach islands out there too have maintained an irresistible lure through the centuries for castaway seekers of soulfulness. Eailean an Naoimhe — island of the saints — was the site of St Brendan's monastery and possibly Columba's spiritual sanctuary where he found his perfect retreat for contemplation. Beehive cells once inhabited by his missionaries still exist and it may even be the site of his mother Eithne's grave.

Tales from Loch Awe
by A C McKerracher

Loch Awe, the River Loch, flows for 24 narrow miles through mid-Argyll, with its waters dotted by tree-clad islets and overshadowed by mighty, mist-capped mountains. Around its shores lie grim, ruined castles, silent reminders of the days when clan fought clan until eventually the race of Campbell emerged triumphant, and dominated all Argyll. The stories and traditions of a thousand years of recorded history were passed down faithfully amongst the local people, from generation to generation, until first translated from the Gaelic and set down in writing last century, and these are a few of the tales of Loch Awe.

Burning of Fincharn Castle

In the early 12th century the lands of Glassary at the south end of Loch Awe were held by a chieftain called Mac Mhic Iain. His castle stood four square on a crag called Fionn-Charn, The Rock of Fion, surrounded on three sides by the waters of the loch. The tower had neither windows nor entrance gate, and when it was built no one can say, but many believe it is the oldest stone-built castle in Scotland.

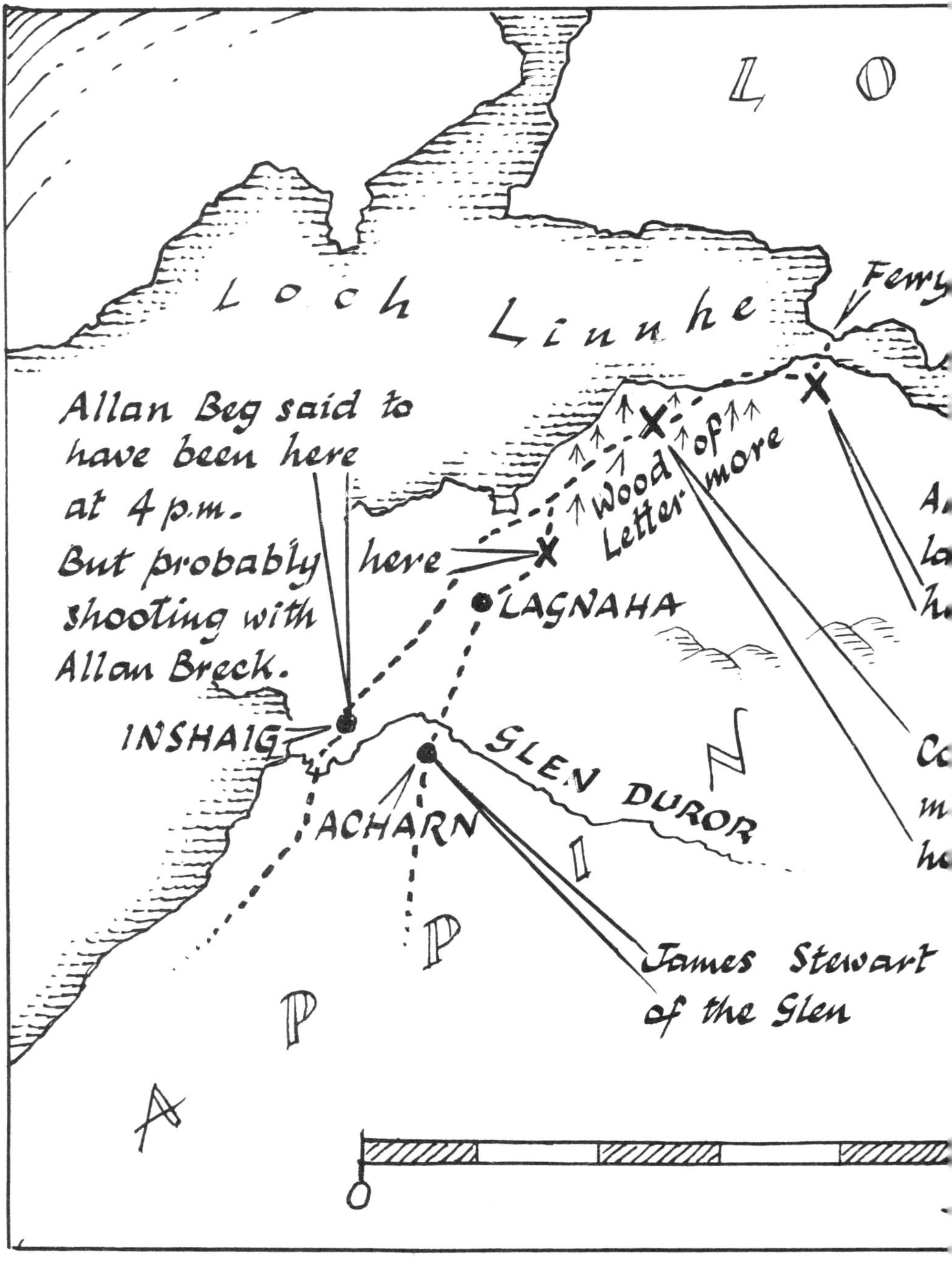

L O

Loch Linnhe

Ferry

Allan Beg said to have been here at 4 p.m. But probably shooting with Allan Breck.

here →

✕ Wood of Lettermore

✕

✕

INSHAIG

● LAGNAHA

ACHARN

GLEN DUROR

James Stewart of the Glen

A P P I N

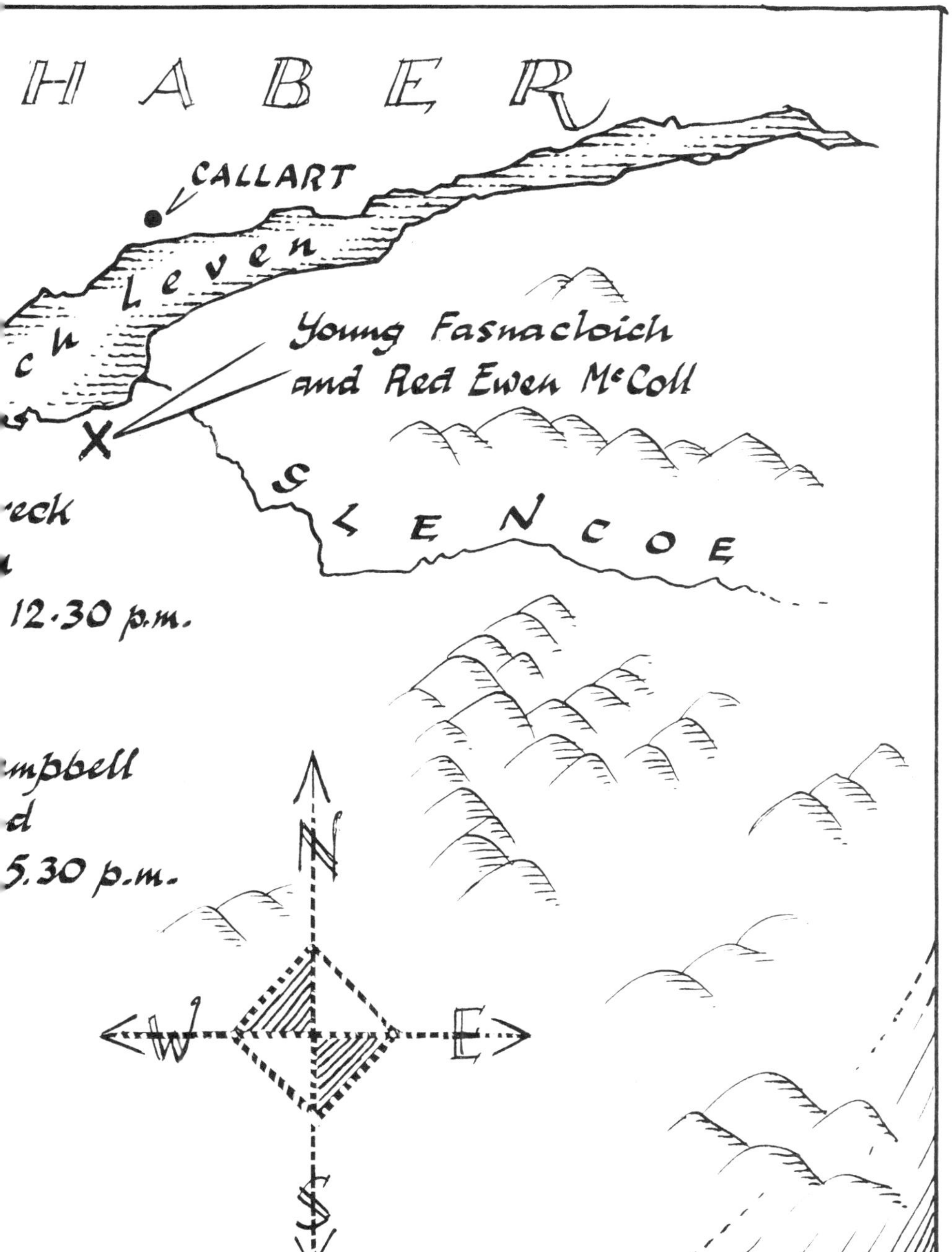

LOCHABER

CALLART

Loch Leven

Young Fasnacloich
and Red Ewen McColl

X

GLENCOE

...reck
...
12.30 p.m.

...mpbell
...d
5.30 p.m.

N W E S

Now Mac Mhic Iain was an arrogant, overbearing chieftain who demanded from his people all the privileges of his position. One of his leading followers had a daughter called Una who fell in love with a neighbouring youth, and great was the joy when their wedding day was named — that is, until Mac Mhic Iain heard the news and declared that on that night he must have his 'rights' as overlord! In vain did Una throw herself at his feet in tears and plead with him. In vain did her father protest that such a barbaric custom had long died out. Mac Mhic Iain refused to listen, and was adamant in his demand.

So the marriage ceremony was a sad affair, and afterwards the guests gathered silently in the nearby wooden hall to eat the wedding feast. Then Mac Mhic Iain came striding in to join them, smiling at the sight of the white clad bride who would be his that night. But a frown darkened his face when he saw the groom was absent, and then came a cry, 'Fire! Fionn-Charn's on fire!' The chief realised immediately what had happened and with an oath flung himself from the hall and raced alone towards his burning castle. He met Una's husband making his escape through the woods by the shore, and a desperate fight took place which ended with Mac Mhic Iain lying on the grass with the youth's sword blade at his throat. He promised to abdicate in exchange for his life, and Fincharn Castle has remained a ruin from that day to this.

The chief's family continued to hold Glassary until 1374 when it passed by marriage to the Scrymgeours who held the lands until 1668 when they lost all their estates and titles through trickery. Their Earldom was restored in 1953 and since then they have re-purchased much of their ancestral lands around Loch Awe.

The battle at the Red Ford

About the time of Fincharn's burning an incomer arrived at the north end of Loch Awe who had a *Cam-Beul*, or crooked mouth. He married the heiress, Eva O'Duine, who brought him a small amount of land locally, and their descendants, still called by their founder's nickname, established themselves in the island castle of Ard Chonnel, mid-way up the loch.

Chailein *Na Cam-Beul*, of the Crooked Mouth, was chief of this minor clan in 1292 when a charter of King John Baliol listed the twelve most important barons in Argyll. This began with Alasdair MacDougall, Lord of Lorn, who held most of Argyll, then followed the MacGregors, MacIvors, MacNaughtons, etc before it finished with Chailein as the smallest landowner. The monks who wrote the charter must have scratched their tonsured heads in puzzlement over his strange name before deciding to render it as 'Colini Cambel'.

This 'Colini Cambel' was dark and swarthy and because of his size his followers dubbed him *Chailein Mor*, Colin the Great, or Mighty. He was also highly ambitious, and in 1296 disputed the boundaries of his land with MacDougall, Lord of Lorn, who dispatched a strong force led by his son John *Brathac*, John the Lame, to overawe this upstart chieftain. It was agreed the peaceful negotiations would take place at a stream still called Allt a' Chomhlachaidh, The Burn of Meeting, on the disputed boundary, high up in the Sreinge (Pass) of Lorn.

The MacDougalls carried with them a magic charm stone to ensure a favourable outcome but as they marched past Loch Scammadale the charm leapt from its custodian's pocket, and vanished beneath the surface of the loch. Some say this strange event was caused by a MacDougall with a premonition that the meeting would not be as peaceful as promised, but, whatever the reason, MacDougall of Raray, Captain of the Clan, refused to proceed any further, and despite Lame John's entreaties the Captain turned for home with his followers.

Meanwhile Colin the Mighty had arrived at the meeting place but finding it deserted had marched further into Lorn. His party had reached as far as the ford over the stream in Finglen before it met the depleted MacDougall force. Recriminations began to fly, followed by verbal abuse which shortly turned to violence, and the clansmen on both sides flung off their plaids, knotted their saffron shirts between their legs, and rushed into battle with their claymores. The slaughter was terrible, and so many died that the surviving fighters could cross and re-cross the burn on the backs of the dead. The water ran red with blood, giving the stream its present name of the Allt Dearg, The Red Burn, while the ford became the Ath Dearg, the Red Ford.

The struggle moved uphill where the Cambel piper stood on a hillock playing his clan to war. Then he saw a piper friend on the MacDougall side fall dead, and in his grief at the death of a fellow musician he composed an impromptu pibroch:

"My loss! my loss! that I have not three hands,
Two engaged with the pipe and one with the sword,
My loss! my loss! low lies yonder,
MacDougall with his pipe, whose sound was soft and sweet to me."

Alas, a Cambel clansman was so enraged at the change of tune that he ran at the piper and cut off his head with one stroke of his claymore. The piper's nerveless fingers played a few more notes on his chanter before his headless body fell to the ground, and the knoll where he stood is called to this day Tom a' Phiobair, The Piper's Hillock.

Chailein Mor stood nearby, watching with satisfaction as the MacDougalls were steadily cut down. The day was almost his when a fleet footed MacDougall scout came slipping over the hill behind, and at the rock called Sgur nan Gillean he notched an arrow to his bow and aimed it carefully. The deadly shaft struck Chailein Mor full in the chest and he fell mortally wounded. The battle ceased immediately. His sorrowful clansmen erected the cairn called Charn Chailein at the spot where their chief had fallen before carrying his body for twelve miles over the mountains for burial at the church of St Peter the Deacon at Kilchrenan.

The Battle at the Red Ford, while seeming a defeat for the race of Cambels, actually marked the beginning of their rise out of obscurity to become Lords of Argyll and the Western Highlands — and almost to rule all Scotland. Chailein Mor was succeeded by his son Neil who had been educated at the Burgh School of Dundee. His closest friend here was a giant lad from Renfrewshire called William Wallace, and when he died a horrible death in London in 1305 Neil was so angered that he was one of the first to join the side of Robert the Bruce. He was later knighted, married the king's sister, and was granted much land after independence was achieved. He took his father's nickname as his patronymic, and became the first *Mac Chailein Mor*, the Son of Great Colin, which since that time has been the Gaelic designation of the chiefs of Clan Campbell, the 'p' being added to their name in the latter half of the 15th century.

The Campbells were quick to realise that more could be achieved with the pen than the sword, and acquired the ancient Lordship of Lorn by marriage in 1470. Thus the flag that flies today over Inveraray Castle, seat of the 28th *Mac Chailein Mor*, bears in two corners the Royal black *galley* of the MacDougalls, once Kings of the Hebrides and Lords of Lorn, while in the other two is the Gyronny of Eight, the arms of Neil Cambel, son of the Great Colin who fell at the Battle of the Red Ford in the Sreinge of Lorn.

The tailor and the Devil

The ruins of Kilneuair Church now lie buried deep in forest, only to be found by taking the old hill path from Ford to Loch Fyne.

Here in a clearing are the remains of a church of astonishing beauty, ornately carved, with an exquisite oratory close by, and both in size and architecture it is unique among West Highland churches. Around it lie ancient tombstones depicting knights in armour, and here sleeps the race of MacPhedrans, Captains of the Campbell war galleys who held the ferry rights of Loch Awe for four hundred years as reward for saving the life of Neil Campbell's son during a storm.

Overhanging the ruin is the skeleton of the tree which gave the church its name, The Church of the Yew, while still inside is the carved, stone baptismal font. Tradition has it that not a stone was dressed on the site but that all masonry was hewed at Killevin on Loch Fyne, and the people of the district formed a twelve mile line over the hills to pass the blocks one by one.

The church fell into ruin after being abandoned in the late Middle Ages when a new chapel was erected at Kilmichael, and later acquired a reputation as an abode of evil spirits which none would pass at night. Into the area came a certain travelling tailor who laughed at such superstitious nonsense, and bragged one night in the inn at Ford that not only would he spend the night within the haunted church, but would make a pair of trews to pass the time.

The locals egged him on, and the tailor found himself seated in the ruin, cursing his boastful tongue, as the hour of midnight approached.

However, he set to work on the trews by the flickering flame from his torch, but scarcely had he started when a deep, hollow voice enquired in Gaelic, "Seest thou this great, hoary hand, tailor?" and a huge, skeletal hand emerged from a nearby grave. "I see that but I will sew this," replied the tailor as boldly as he could. The voice spoke again. "Seest thou this large, grey head, tailor?" as an evil head appeared from the shadows. "I see that but I will sew this," quavered the wretched tailor, trying to concentrate on his stitches.

This conversation continued until all the members of an inhuman body had appeared and assembled themselves together. With a yell of terror the tailor leapt from his seat and dived through the door. A huge hand tried to grab him but missed and struck the wall, and the outline of that ghostly handprint can still be seen, etched for eternity upon the stone of Kilneuair Church.

Goc Am Go

At the birth in 1605 of Alasdair MacCholla MacDonald, son of old Coll *Ciotich* of Colonsay, every sword in the house rattled in its scabbard and all the locks snapped off the guns. His superstitious father would have had him drowned immediately, but the nurse, a Wise Woman, persuaded him the signs were for good, not evil. Alasdair grew into a ferocious youth, able to tear apart a bull's carcass with his bare hands, for in his veins ran the blood of Conn of the Hundred Battles and of Viking *berserkers*. When he came of age his old nurse burned a blue thread in a kiln, and peering into the smoke predicted he would perform mighty deeds and be successful in all things, but that his downfall would occur when a silver coin leapt from his banner, and he met with Gocam-Go. Alasdair laughed aloud in the arogance of youth, for when was there ever a Gocam-Go, or Spy, amongst kinsfolk.

Around 1639 Alasdair and his father were driven from their Colonsay homeland by the avaricious Campbells, and the son took refuge with his kin in Ireland, the MacDonnells of Antrim. Here he brooded until 1644 when he learnt that James Graham, the Great Marquis of Montrose, had raised an army for Charles I against the Covenanters, and he saw in this the means of his revenge.

Alasdair joined Montrose at Blair Castle in Atholl in August, 1644, along with 600 fighting men from Ireland. He was then aged forty, a giant of a man nearly seven feet tall, with red, shaggy hair and long, drooping moustaches. He was prone to heavy drinking, sullen moods, and sudden violence but his bravery was already legend. A curious bond developed between the slender, intellectual Marquis, and Alasdair Mac-Cholla, the politically naive, savage, fighting man from a bygone age. Together they carved a place in Scotland's history during the Annus Mirabilis of 1644-45 when, with only a small force, they won a series of victories at Tippermuir, Fyvie, Inverlochy, Auldearn and Kilsyth. Alasdair was knighted and created Major-General of the King's army, and his great, two-handed claymore was to the fore in every battle. Being ambidextrous like his father he acquired the same nickname, Cholla *Ciotich,* the Left Handed One, which the terrified Lowlanders altered to 'Colkitto', and they used it to frighten unruly children for generations to come.

After the Battle of Kilsyth, Alasdair led his men north to harry the lands of his hated Campbell enemies, leaving Montrose's depleted force to be cut to pieces at Philiphaugh by a Covenanting army under General David Leslie. During the years 1646-7 he carved a swathe of destruction through Argyll, leaving it like a desert, and his enemies gave him another name, Alasdair MacCholla, 'The Devastator'. However, he failed to break the Campbell castles, and on 21st May, 1647, the army of Leslie and Argyll arrived at Inveraray.

Alasdair rallied his forces at the south end of Loch Awe where his standard bearer planted his flag on a hill behind Ford, and, as the shaft hit the ground, a silver coin sprang up. Unaware of this strange event, Alasdair advanced to the narrow pass beside Loch Ederline to find it blocked by a party of local people commanded by Zachary Mor MacCallum, chief of Clan Malcolm. Alasdair, impressed by such determination, uttered the now classic phrase, "None remained loyal to Campbell but stone and lime and MacCallum", and suggested a single combat.

Both sides grounded their weapons to watch this classic meeting for Zachary Mor was also noted as a master swordsman. The two blades rose and fell as the fighters circled and parried, and Alasdair stopped several times to compliment MacCallum on a skilful move. However, there was no doubt about the outcome for Alasdair MacCholla, 'The Red Handed Horse Knight' was renowned as the most ferocious swordsman in all of Gaeldom.

The blades continued to meet and clash until suddenly a sword spun through the air, and a great gasp arose. Alasdair stared dumbfounded at his empty sword hand, then turned white faced to the equally astonished MacCallum. "What place is this?" he whispered. "Why, Goc Am Go", came the surprised reply, "the False Outlet, where once the waters of Loch Awe drained to the sea from the south." Alasdair staggered back in horror, realising he had misheard his old nurse, and that what she had said was Goc-Am-Go, not Gocam-Go. But still reluctant to believe, he took a charm stone from his pocket and flung it over the heads of his troops. Always had this been found before but now it fell into the muddy reeds and disappeared.

Alasdair rallied his force in silence, and drove south into Kintyre with the devil behind him — leaving historians to puzzle ever since why he failed to hold the easily defended, narrow isthmus at Tarbert. He left three hundred men to garrison Dunaverty Castle at the mull of Kintyre, and took passage in a boat, with his terror so great that he hacked off the fingers of those who clung to the gunwales and might delay him. From here he fled to Gigha, then to Islay, where he left another party commanded by his seventy-seven year old father to hold Dunnyveg Castle. All of those left behind were to die later after surrendering on honourable terms. Now Alasdair fled to Antrim, trying to escape his fate, and here, on the 21st of

November, 1647, he was treacherously stabbed to death in the back. Sir Alasdair MacCholla 'Ciotich' MacDonald, Major-General of Montrose's army, whom history books call 'Colkitto', whom the Campbells called 'The Devastator' but who all Gaeldom honoured as 'The Red Handed Horse Knight', had finally met his Goc-Am-Go, at the False Outlet of Loch Awe.

The armourers of Argyll

The Campbells first acquired the ancestral MacGregor lands at the head of Loch Awe by marriage in 1320. They sealed this later by legal charter, and gradually the Gregors were squeezed out and forced to depart to Balquhidder, Glen Lyon and Rannoch. Some were retained for their services, like the branch of MacAne MacGregors who were appointed hereditary keepers of the new Campbell castle of Kilchurn when it was built in 1440. Also retained was a family of MacNabs who were noted smiths and armourers, and lived at Barr a' Chastalein above Dalmally. They provided the ironwork for the castle, and were appointed hereditary armourers to the Knights of Lochawe, furnishing them with coats of chain mail, swords, targes and pistols over the centuries. They continued in office even after the Campbells of Glenorchy had moved their residence east to Loch Tay, for *The Black Book of Taymouth* records that in 1620 Patrick, son of the smith, was ordered to appear and answer for his irascible disposition.

However, after the 45, there was little demand for armourers, and the MacNab family became purely blacksmiths. When Thomas Pennant visited Dalmally during his famous Tour of Scotland in 1769 he recorded his meeting with this renowned family of smiths who had carried on their work without a break for 369 years. There too came Thomas Leyden during his tour, and found two MacNab brothers living at Barr a

Chastalein who proudly showed him rusty chain mail, helmets and targes made by their predecessors.

Here too came the renowned Gaelic poet, Duncan Ban MacIntyre, with a beautiful horn taken from a wild goat which he desired to be made into a sgian dubh. MacNab the Smith put all his skill into the work, and when it was finished the poet was delighted. "How much do I owe you?" he asked, to which MacNab replied, "Money could not buy its like. Make a verse about it, and as masters of our crafts we shall both be served." And Duncan Ban did compose a poem in praise of MacNab the Smith and the knife he had wrought.

A tradition in these parts said that the MacNab smiths would cease to be when an elm tree fell at Barr a' Chastalein, and when the last actual smith lay dying about the end of the eighteenth century a storm arose and blew down an ancient elm across the doorway. Inside lay dead the last armourer whose family had served the Campbells of Glenorchy for nearly four hundred years.

The MacNabs continued to live at Barr a Chastalein, but not as smiths, until the beginning of this century when the last of them moved away. The writer's mother remembers seeing him as a venerable, white-bearded gentleman around 1914 when he made one of his frequent visits to his birthplace where his family had lived for five hundred years. Today the hamlet of Barr a' Chastalein consists only of low, ruined walls, fast sinking into a new forestry plantation, but beside it lies a mound of iron slag, the only monument to a race of famous smiths.

The curse on McColl's grave
by Monica Henderson-Atkinson

Iron railings surround McColl's grave by the old ruined church in the ancient graveyard on a hillside overlooking Kilchoan in Ardnamurchan. To this day the grave is a fearsome sight, covered with heavy weeds which grow rampant, not through neglect, but as a result of the curse placed upon the occupant last century by my great-grandmother.

Lush grass covers most of the graveyard, but it stops short at McColl's grave and whereas the other graves are, in the main, quite neatly and tidily kept with interesting headstones, even on a warm September afternoon a shivery feeling came over us as my husband and I stood by this monstrosity.

It was when we were on holiday at Kilchoan that I followed up the story of the curse which Ann-Margaret Henderson laid upon the luckless McColl, who was the Tackman and Agent acting for John James Dalgleish, the proprietor of Ardnamurchan.

At the end of May, 1886, John and Ann-Margaret Henderson were evicted from their croft. John had had money worries and had refused to pay any more rent for his little farm. He also made a stand in the Tobermory Court against paying dues for road money, as the Road Trustees would not erect a bridge across the river leading to his farm. The Trustees were just as adamant that they would not erect a bridge over the river until John had paid his rent and dues. Stalemate!

The proprietor, John James Dalgleish, refused to renew the lease of the farm because Henderson had taken up the crofters' cause (this was just before the Crofting Act became law) and Dalgleish was determined to evict his obstreperous tenant before he inflamed the others.

John put up a strong resistance to the eviction, repulsing all attempts to drive himself, his wife and six young children out of their home. Finally a Messenger-at-Arms with six commissioners and the Court Officer were despatched from Oban to evict the family. This body of men arrived at Tobermory but found that nobody would transport them across to Kilchoan and nobody at Kilchoan would come to Tobermory for them. However, they finally found one man who would. His name was Duncan Cameron and he set out from Kilchoan to collect them in his skiff. So strong was the feeling in the district that he dare not land the squad of evictors at the Kilchoan slipway but took them three or four miles farther on to an isolated bay called MacLean's Nose. From there the party made their way to the Hendersons' croft.

It was no surprise that it was Duncan Cameron who assisted the eviction party as, in the preceding two or three years, there had been numerous flare-ups between him and John. On several occasions, John had complained to the Kirk Session of the Free Church of harassment by Duncan Cameron, and had once lodged a complaint that Cameron "feloniously, wickedly and malignantly assaulted me last night on board the steamer *Pioneer*".

On enquiring further, the Moderator was told by John that Cameron had tried to push him overboard by seizing him around his waist and pushing him against the side of the boat, to the risk of his life. John's eldest son, Angus, was called and upon his word of honour before the Moderator said that he saw Duncan Cameron wrestling with his father and pushing him about in the boat.

It appears that the two crofters were like chalk and cheese and would never get on together.

Once in Kilchoan, the eight men successfully achieved the eviction of the Henderson family, watched by McColl. One can imagine the scene at the little croft as the neighbours stood around, unable to help but more probably adding their protests as the men brought out John, Ann-Margaret and the six children. Ann-Margaret was ill in bed at the time and had to be carried out on a litter. Records state that two doctors certified that she could safely be removed from the house although she was too ill to walk. The family were deposited on the shore above the high-water mark, surrounded by their possessions, with only an old tent for shelter.

It was as she was being taken from her cottage that Ann-Margaret pointed her finger at McColl and laid the curse upon him. Evidently she regarded him as the person most responsible for depriving the family of their home. There is no reason to think that he was particularly elderly, being employed full-time as a bailiff, but she prophesied "bad cess" to him and said that he would soon die and when he was dead and buried the very grass would not grow on his grave, only docks and nettles.

Sure enough McColl did die shortly afterwards and was laid to rest in the ancient graveyard at Kilchoan. Grass was sown on his grave but it withered and died and in its place grew huge ugly dock leaves and nettles. His relations weeded it again and again and planted more grass-seed, but still the dock leaves and nettles crawled all over the grave. The ground was dug over, cleared and covered with new turf but it was no use — the docks and nettles returned even more strongly. I am told that every possible effort has been made to keep down the weeds, but all endeavours have been in vain.

Records in *Hansard* of the 17th May, 1886, state that Mr MacFarlane, MP for Argyll, asked J B Balfour, the Lord Advocate, if his attention had been called to the eviction of a tenant named John Henderson, in Ardnamurchan, by a body of men while Henderson's wife was unwell.

It was disclosed that the family were offered a house in Tobermory rent-free for a year. This was refused, as was an offer of temporary accommodation in an inn at Kilchoan.

It seems that Dalgleish was extremely eager to obtain the

Henderson croft by any means and it was obviously a sop to his conscience to offer the alternative accommodation.

John's eldest son, my great-uncle Angus, had memories of the older crofters in the Highlands being affected by "writs of removal" which were served on them by landlords greedy for land on which to breed sheep for meat and wool. The landlords would stop at nothing to hound their poor tenants to give up their little crofts, even though, in the main, the crofters were good farmers. Their life was an unenviable one with the Sword of Damocles always hanging overhead and many of them had to eke out their scanty livelihood by taking other jobs, as John had done by acting as Piermaster at Mingary.

Great-uncle Angus told me of many clashes which took place and of the pitched battles which ensued between the crofters, landlords agents, police and troops, skirmishes in which skulls were cracked and arms and legs broken.

Later on, in the year that John and Ann-Margaret were callously evicted, the Crofters (Scotland) Act gave them their rights of security of tenancy and fair rents, as a Royal Commission sided with the crofters. By this time, however, **thousands had perished from starvation, injuries and diseases and thousands more had emigrated with many of them ending up on the Falkland Islands.**

The Henderson family lived in their tent on the shore for about six weeks before arrangements were made to transport them and their belongings to Skye where Ann-Margaret owned some property. One wonders why they were not taken in by neighbours, but perhaps the other crofters were afraid of repercussions if they harboured the unrepentant and rebellious crusader. The second eldest child, Thomas Carswell Henderson, my grandfather, remembered kind neighbours bringing them broth and home-baked bread.

It's interesting that Thomas's father should have been such a rebel, for over a generation later, Thomas married into the family of that very rebellious and forthright lady — Mrs Emmeline Pankhurst!

After our holiday in Kilchoan we, too, left for the Isle of Skye. We wanted to see where John and Ann-Margaret had been finally laid to rest. Their story had a happy ending as they'd been very contented on Skye and made a success of farming their own croft.

We drove to Trumpan up the long hill to the small ruined church. It used to have a thatched roof, but in the 16th century the building was set alight by the MacDonalds, killing many MacLeods who were worshipping at the time.

Many members of my family had described the ruined church, but words cannot describe how utterly dramatic is the scene at Trumpan. The church stands high on a headland on the Waternish peninsula looking out across the Little Minch above the restless Atlantic on three sides while to the rear are hills covered with sheep, their bleating mingling with the crashing sound of the waves far below. It's all so wild and beautiful and far from the turmoil of the world.

There it was — near the gateway to the churchyard, the largest gravestone of them all, an obelisk towering high above the grave of my great-grandparents. John built this dramatic memorial himself, bringing cement, stones, sand and water up the hill in a little cart and after much hard labouring erecting this outstanding monument to Ann-Margaret.

The words John carved on the gravestone are very formal: "To the memory of Mrs Henderson". They may sound cold to the casual observer, but I have been told by older members of the family that John was a man of great sensitivity and, being proud of the fact that he had married a descendant of the Roxburghe Innes family, he probably thought it only right and proper to carve a respectful epitaph on such a monumental (in every respect) gravestone to a lady with such noble antecedents.

A few years later, John was laid to rest with his Ann-Margaret, so now they are together, at peace at last after their turbulent life in Kilchoan. The family grave is well-kept and tidy with John's name carved underneath that of his wife. One of their grandsons and family reside in the property formerly owned by Ann-Margaret, in a beautiful spot about two miles from the churchyard. As we drove from The Old Stein, as the property is named, up the hill to Trumpan we thought of John, all those years ago, labouring along with the little cart and materials for building the gravestone. No motorised transport then and we have been told that he did not use a horse to pull the cart. What devotion he was showing to his dearly beloved Ann-Margaret! I am not ashamed to say I put my arms round the gravestone and shed a few tears of love and pride for the great-grandparents I had never known.

When Ian, one of John and Ann-Margaret's great-grandsons, died in an accident at a tragically early age he was buried near their grave. A Pipe-Major from the 1st Battalion Scots Guards, Ian's old regiment, came up to Trumpan and in full dress uniform walked slowly round the churchyard, playing laments. No-one could wish for more than to be played home at the end.

The battle of Campbeltown
by Jane A McCusker

It was a summer's morning in 1813, and the folk of Campeltown were busily going about their everyday business. Few noticed the *Maria,* a small naval vessel, anchored off the pier. No one, it seems, realised that she was an armed tender, employed specifically on impress service.

Craft such as these collected press-ganged men at rendezvous points and delivered them to receiving ships. The men were put into the holds which were then securely battened down.

Conditions in these press tenders were notoriously bad, and the filth and overcrowding made them mainly responsible for the high incidence of typhus fever then widespread in the fleet. Once on board a tender, and sealed in with numerous other unfortunates, an impressed man was beyond rescue or escape.

A longboat set out from the *Maria,* and made for the shore. In charge was Midshipman James Henry and he had orders to seize any man who might make a sailor, and to drag him away from his family, home, and friends.

For the teenage officer, impressment duty must have seemed rather inglorious, but it was necessary. This was the time of the Napoleonic Wars. Trafalgar had been fought in 1805, less than eight years before, and it was during this crisis period that impressment was at its height. Most of the Navy's needs were met by volunteers, but every year an additional requirement of 2,000 unfortunate men were compelled to serve by brute force. Such enforced recruitment was hated, feared, and often violently opposed.

Midshipman Henry must have thought himself very lucky that day, for he and his crew landed quietly and without incident, rapidly seized six men, and began to head back for their boat. It was then things began to happen.

The town had been alerted. Word spread quickly that the press-gang had struck, and in *Commentaries on the Law of Scotland Respecting Crimes* written by Baron David Hume, it is reported that young James Henry suddenly found himself and his crew "opposed by a riotous crowd of people, who collected against them, armed with sticks, stones, bricks and other like weapons, with which they commenced a violent attack on him and his party, calling out to each other, to 'murder the pressing vagabonds'."

Despite its restrained language, the passage goes on to capture the terrifying confusion of the desperate battle:

"Several of the party received severe blows, and were brought to the ground. A marine was beaten down, and his side-arms were nearly wrested from him; one or two pistols were fired at them from windows in the town; and three of the impressed men were forcibly rescued. On this occasion, an officer of the party fired his pistol in return; and Henry was heard at this time repeatedly to call out, 'For God's sake not to fire among the mob, but over their heads'."

Bloodied and bruised, the sailors fought their way to the boat and rowed back to the *Maria*. Only then was it discovered that one of their number, William Johnston, had been left behind. Hume wrote: "This man had received a cut, and been knocked down, and disabled from keeping up with the party; and he thus fell into the power of the multitude, who were so exasperated on the occasion, that even after he was carried into a house, many of them followed him in and violently threatened his life, till assured he was not an officer, but a private seaman only."

The magistrates decided that they had to protect Johnston, and hastily attempted to rescue him. They carried and dragged him to the head of the pier and hailed the *Maria* to collect their man.

Midshipman Henry was put in charge of the boat for the return journey, but as it was thought to be a trap, two marines went with the party. Ironically, two of the captured impressed men were judged unsuitable, and were also to return to freedom.

The whole episode had been an unmitigated disaster for the Navy. The people of Campbeltown had successfully saved five of the six local men, and had trounced the press-gang so severely that a return visit would be unlikely.

For young James Henry, the incident was particularly humiliating. He had been attacked, frightened, and in the heat of the moment, seen one of his men almost shoot into a crowd of townspeople. Now they had lost one of their own men and he had to go back and retrieve him. He sat at the helm and tried to hide his nervousness as he steered towards the pier.

Hume's account of Henry's second visit emphasises the youth's fear and confusion. He wrote: "Among others who were prepossessed with the belief that the hailing had been a mere decoy, was Henry himself; and in his opinion he was confirmed by the reception the party met with on approaching the shore. Not knowing of a landing-place at the head of the pier, where the magistrates and Johnston were, Henry pushed farther on, for the stairs at the middle of the pier; and here the mob again presented themselves, shouting and threatening and throwing a great many stones at the party in the boat."

As the stones splashed around them, the marines fired four times over the heads of the people. Henry shouted repeatedly that next time he must, and would give orders to fire at them, but the Campbeltown folk were enjoying their victory at the expense of the frightened boy who did not seem to know what to do next. They laughed and jeered, and others soon came to join in the fun as Henry's boat bobbed ridiculously in front of them.

Henry had his orders to find Johnston, and he feared losing more men to this mob. His crew waited for a decision. In desperation, "Henry took the musket from the marine, and fired three times successively on the multitude. Upon the last shot, they were observed immediately to disperse."

Henry put the two freed men ashore, and then discovered that while he had been confronting the mob, Johnston had been sent back in another boat from the head of the pier. He hastily returned to the *Maria*.

Later, while he was recovering, he received a stunning blow. News came that one of his shots had hit a 15-year-old girl who had now died. He was told that he faced a murder charge, and possibly hanging.

The prosecution later dropped the murder charge, but the court held that Henry was guilty of culpable homicide. The jury, though, had compassion. According to Hume, they "considered the violence and obstinacy of the assault, the great patience of the seamen in the first stages of it, the personal injuries recently sustained, and the many warnings given the mob without effect."

No doubt they also considered the extreme youthfulness of the prisoner as he stood, shocked and pale, before them. The jury brought in a verdict of justifiable homicide and young James Henry went free.

In the Battle of Campbeltown, a girl had been killed, a midshipman tried for murder, several sailors had been severely beaten, and all the Navy had gained was one unwilling conscript!

Columba's secret cave
by Charles Tennant

Until a recent summer I had visited Loch Caolisport only once and that was in the year 1925 when I arrived in the loch by sea as a young and very inexperienced yachtsman. With three friends,

I had sailed from the Clyde in a broad-beamed, gaff-rigged cutter *The Boudjah,* which we had chartered from the piermaster at Rhu. After being very seasick off the Mull of Kintyre, waiting for the floodtide to help us northward, we were thankful to find a sheltered anchorage in the lee of an island lying off the west shore of Loch Caolisport. Our charts told us it was Eilean Na Uamhaidh, "The Island of the Cave".

We were very conscious that we had sailed the same stormy seas by which the early Christian missionaries such as St Columba had come from Ireland in less seaworthy vessels than our own, and we had a fellow feeling for their zeal.

The cave is not on the island but some distance up from the shore facing it. Locally it is known as Columba's Cave and tradition has it that the saint occcupied it during a visit to King Conal, the Pictish ruler of Dalriada. Before the arrival of Columba, however, a number of Christian Irish Scotti had established themselves among the pagan Picts on the coast of Argyll and it is possible that some of them used the cave.

When I revisited the area I arrived by car, and was surprised to find that so little public notice is given to the cave. The approach is by the quiet, single-track road along the lochside and, with the sea having long receded from the original coastline, the cave is now some 100 yards above the high water line and invisible from the road. At a point where a bay faces out to the island, on the right hand side of the road a rough sign sticks up through the bracken, bearing the one word CAVE. From the foot of the post, a track led us through the bracken past derelict buildings including the gable-end of a mediaeval chapel, to the cave entrance. Being no longer lapped by the waves, it appears as a cleft in the hillside, with another small cave alongside.

As we entered, and our eyes became accustomed to the dark, its use in olden days as a Christian sanctuary became apparent. There is an altar built up from the floor with loose stones and, above it, cut into the sloping roof, a rough Latin cross, seven inches in height. Below the altar, scooped out of the rock floor, are two hollow bowls which may well have been used as sacred vessels for the administration of the Sacrament.

It is the cross, the emblem of the Christian church, cut into the solid wall of the cave, and the fact that this carving has survived in its original state, which gives the cave its charm and makes its discovery a moment to remember. A visitor cannot help feeling the influence of the early Christians who made the cave a place of worship so many centuries ago.

One expert dates the cross to the 11th century, but that is not to say the cave was not used by Christians much earlier. If, as is said, Columba visited the Pictish King Conal, it would have been at Caisteal an Torr, the Fortress of the Tower, at the head of Loch Caolisport, of which nothing remains today except a heap of stones. The purpose of the meeting was to ask for royal assent to the foundation of a Christian monastery in Iona.

Archaeologists tell us that finds made at the cave show it was used as a human habitation from prehistoric times.

The spread of the Christian gospel from the islands of Iona, Eilach an Naoimh in the Garvellachs, and from Lismore to the mainland peninsulas of Keills and Kilmory, where ancient chapels remain, is sparsely documented. There is, however, considerable evidence to be seen of the way of life in these primitive days from the stone carvings which have been collected in the Chapel of St Maelrubha, another early missionary saint, at Kilmory. This chapel lies just over the hill from the cave in Loch Caolisport at the entrance to Loch Sween, and there are more stones outside the Chapel of Keills on the north side of this loch.

The carvings show Christian knights in armour carrying broadswords as large as themselves, wild animals, and sailing vessels in which no modern yachtsman would venture far from shore.

Of all these carvings, the cross in the cave in Loch Caolisport is the most significant to me. Perhaps due to its position in the curved roof of the cave, it has been preserved throughout the centuries from the depredation of researchers as well as from vandals, and brings the visitor in touch with a time and way of life long gone.

The absence of tourist bus parties and the quietness of the single-track roads make a visit to the cave and the Chapels of St Maelrubha and Keills a rare pleasure. There is time here to contemplate the arrival of Christianity in this part of Scotland against a background of sea lochs, islands, mountains and scenery of a beauty which remains constant from generation to generation.

Framed for murder to crush Jacobite spirit

When Colin Campbell of Glenure was shot by an assassin on 14 May 1752, a Highland legend was born. Mystery and controversy have surrounded the incident ever since. *Archie McKerracher* cites fresh evidence which, he believes, reveals the killer at last.

Who committed the Appin murder — and why — has been the greatest unsolved mystery in Highland history. It has the added fascination in the claim that the secret of the murderer's identity is said to have been passed down through an Appin family to the present day.

For many years, all writers on the subject have had to draw their information from the published account of the trial at which James Stewart was convicted of the murder of Colin

Campbell of Glenure. This has been the only source available, for all other records were deliberately destroyed as soon as the case was finished.

In recent years, however, one surviving record of the precognitions (the statements taken from witnesses to establish if there are grounds for prosecution) of 120 witnesses has come to light in the Advocates' Library of the National Library of Scotland. Most of them were not called upon to testify, but their statements make appalling reading. They reveal that the prosecution knew James Stewart was innocent of the murder before the trial began; that the jury was not biased as has often been suggested, but that the evidence presented to it was deliberately falsified; and that many of the witnesses lied in court, either deliberately or through fear. Lastly, they also reveal that the circumstances of the murder are quite different from the official account of the trial, around which Robert Louis Stevenson wrote his classic novel, *Kidnapped.*

Unfortunately for tradition, the precognitions also destroy much of the mythology surrounding the murder.

From my researches, it is clear far more lies behind the case than is apparent. James Stewart may have been tried for the murder, but in reality he was hanged for treason. It also seems apparent the murder was either planned, or connived at, in Government offices in Edinburgh. Further, it appears the murderer came neither from Appin nor Lochaber, but Balquhidder.

Stevenson admitted that *Kidnapped* was fiction based on fact, but the novel's popularity has created wide misconception to the present day. Read any book on the area and you will find it stated that "Colin Campbell of Glenure — commonly called 'The Red Fox' — was the Government Factor on the forfeited estates. He evicted a number of Stewarts from their better lands and supplanted them with his Campbell friends. One of the Stewarts evicted and put on poorer land was James Stewart of the Glens." Now, all that is untrue.

Firstly, Colin Campbell of Glenure was never known as "The Red Fox". Stevenson picked up the nickname from a witness at the trial who was coerced into saying that Allan Breck Stewart's drunken remark about bringing him the skin of a red fox must have meant Colin Campbell. This is the only time in history the phrase was ever uttered, and yet it has stuck.

In reality, Colin Campbell was a fair, just and honourable man. In 1748, aged 43, he found employment as Government Factor on the forfeited estates of Mamore and Callart, belonging respectively to the exiled Cameron of Lochiel, and Cameron of Callart. He later added the estate of Ardsheal in Appin, belonging to the exiled Charles Stewart of Ardsheal. He was paid £10.10s.7½d per annum for a thankless and difficult job which he had taken only to occupy his time.

Stevenson portrayed him as a ruthless oppressor, trying to replace the Stewarts with Hanoverian supporters. In fact, Colin Campbell was himself under official suspicion of having Jacobite sympathies and was on the verge of being dismissed. In November 1748, he had appointed a local man, James Stewart, as his sub-factor on the Ardsheal estate. James was a small man, then 53, and the illegitimate half-brother of the exiled Ardsheal. He had been "out" with the Appin regiment in the Forty-Five, but had been pardoned and had settled down on his farm of Auchindarroch in Glen Duror. He was highly respected as a God-fearing man of integrity, and was called James of the Glen — not *Glens,* as many have it — simply to distinguish him from others of that name. The partnership worked well, with Colin Campbell turning a blind eye to the double rent James collected for his exiled chief and kinsman.

In July 1751, Colin Campbell received instructions from the Barons of Exchequer that on no account was he to let any part of a forfeited estate to a relation of the exiled person, nor to any who had not taken the Oath of Allegiance. This had been expected, for he had been reprimanded for doing just that on the Cameron estates. James Stewart came into the first category, and to avoid embarrassing his friend, Campbell, he voluntarily left his farm to move half a mile to the farm of Aucharn on the estate of Campbell of Airds. He was *not* evicted, but reached a private agreement with the incoming tenant, Campbell of Ballievolan, who even agreed to pay an extra rent on behalf of the exiled Ardsheal.

In April 1752, Colin Campbell decided he had no option but to evict some tenants from the Ardsheal estate. However, it was not the mass eviction Stevenson described when he wrote, "The kindly folk of the district must all pack and tramp, every father's son out of every father's house". In fact, only five tenants were involved and all were recent incomers. They were three Colquhouns, a MacColl and a McCorquodale. They had been let farms by James Stewart, but none had taken the Oath of Allegiance.

Colin Campbell had no option but to evict them, though he softened the blow by arranging for them to stay on as stockmen. In any case, everyone knew the removals were only a formality. Control of the estates was about to pass to the Crown Commissioners who would, without doubt, have reinstated the five who were all keen to take the Oath and pay a higher rent.

It is necessary to re-state this to show that while there was some local animosity about the unfairness of the evictions, there was hardly sufficient hatred to kill Colin Campbell. The other Stewart lairds around the small Ardsheal estate — Appin, Lagnaha, Fasnacloich, Ballachulish and Invernahyle — had all been pardoned and remained on their land so *they* had no quarrel with Colin Campbell. The situation was different in Lochaber where memories of Hanoverian atrocities still lingered, and here Campbell was regarded as a traitor because his mother was a Cameron.

It is at this time that Allan Breck Stewart enters the scene. He was far from the romantic Highlander portrayed by Stevenson. He had been fostered by James Stewart, but grew up into a dissolute, pock-marked and knock-kneed youth who squandered his small inheritance in the Appin inns. He had fled the district, leaving his foster-father to pay his bills, and enlisted in the Essex Regiment. He fought at Prestonpans where he deserted to the Jacobites, and after Culloden escaped to France. He had returned to Appin several times to collect the extra rents for Ardsheal, and on the last occasion arrived in Edinburgh in February 1752. From there he made a tour of the leading Stewart families in Menteith and Perthshire before arriving in Appin at the beginning of April. Here he had a meeting with James Stewart and borrowed some clothes to replace his gaudy French uniform before leaving to visit his birthplace in Rannoch.

Shortly after, on 3rd April, James Stewart also left Appin, ostensibly to go to Edinburgh to plead the cause of the evicted tenants, but he did so without consulting any of them or seeking their approval. His journey was a strange one, for on the way, he called on every prominent Jacobite family in Stirlingshire and south Perthshire. He eventually arrived in Ediburgh five days later on 8th April. His return journey was even stranger, for he saw Jacobite families in Stirling, Dunblane, and Alloa and revisited others before returning to Appin on 27th April.

To explain this protracted journey, it is necessary to remember that at this time, another, better-planned, Jacobite Uprising was imminent, and the West Highlands were bubbling like a cauldron. The Elibank Plot — involving the murder of the Hanoverian Royal Family and the seizure of the Tower of London — was set for six months hence. It seems quite clear the Appin evictions were an ideal opportunity for James Stewart, in his capacity as leader of the Stewarts, to travel without suspicion to co-ordinate the Jacobites after detailed information had been relayed to him by Allan Breck.

A fortnight after James arrived back, Colin Campbell of Glenure left Fort William on 14th May 1752, to carry out the Appin evictions. He was accompanied by his 24-year-old nephew Mungo Campbell; Donald Kennedy, a Sheriff's Officer; and his 19-year-old servant, John McKenzie. It is recorded in *The Highland Papers* that his assassination was planned to take place at North Ballachulish in Lochaber, but was foiled by John McKenzie, riding close to his master. Evidence given at James Stewart's trial confirmed there was a murder plot afoot, the instigator of which was said to be James Cameron of Callart.

(The Camerons were appalled when they learned the murder had taken place in Appin. They offered to rescue James Stewart on his way to the gallows, but he refused on the grounds it would only cause more suffering.)

About 5 pm the party safely crossed by the Ballachulish ferry, and Glenure is reputed to have exclaimed, "At last I am safe, now that I am out of my mother's country". The party entered the wood of Lettermore and because of the narrow path, Donald Kennedy rode ahead followed by Mungo and then Colin Campbell. John McKenzie had fallen behind to retrieve a dropped coat and was further delayed by a conversation with one John Roy Livingstone. This delay may have been deliberate.

Suddenly, a shot was fired at Colin Campbell at point blank range from behind a bush. He was hit in the back by two balls and dropped in his saddle. Mungo Campbell was first on the scene, and as he stated at James Stewart's trial, "He saw, at some distance from him, a man going up the hill, wearing a short, dark-coloured coat and trousers and with a gun in his hand". The prosecution claimed this was the murderer, that it was Allan Breck, disguised in James Stewart's clothes.

Stewart was arrested as an accessory to murder on 16th May, purely on the supposed evidence about the clothing. At his trial in Inveraray in September, witness after witness testified that, all the time he was in Appin, Allan Breck had worn a dark short coat with silver buttons, and black and white striped trousers, and that these belonged to Stewart. Upon this evidence hinged most of the prosecution case.

The precognitions tell quite a different story. Mungo Campbell, when questioned just three days after the murder, testified that he had observed a man with a gun in his hand clothed in a short dun coat and breeches who was too far up the hill at the time to be the murderer. He also stated that, from the situation, and his uncle's dying words, he believed two people were involved. This description of a man wearing a short brown coat and knee breeches bears absolutely no resemblance to the clothing worn by Allan Breck and allegedly lent to him by James Stewart, nor could the person going up the hill have been the assassin. Thus the entire prosecution case would have been destroyed if Mungo Campbell had told the truth at the trial.

Even more sinister, he was also the only witness not called upon to identify James Stewart's clothing in court, and yet he was the only person to have seen the alleged murderer.

James Stewart's servants had been put in fear of their lives, and sadly, they, too, lied in court about events after the murder. The prosecution already knew Stewart was innocent of murder, but any witness who might have destroyed their case was not called, and out of nearly 700 people examined, only a handful gave testimony in court. The defence was given no access to any of the statements. For reasons explained later, it is evident the authorities had decided James Stewart had to die at all costs.

As to the famous secret of the murderer's identity — it is quite clear from the discovered statements that there was far more evidence against Allan Beg, James Stewart's eldest son, than against his father, for it was *his* clothes, not his father's, that Allan Breck borrowed. There is also a mystery as to the whereabouts of Allan Beg at the time of the murder, for both his father and his younger brother Charles made conflicting statements. It is clear it was not known where Allan was between 4 pm and 6.30 pm. An informer placed in the same cell at Fort William as James Stewart's servants stated he heard them say Allan Beg should be pitied, and that he would be hanged as well as his father. Another informer said some of the servants were openly saying it was Allan Beg who had murdered Colin Campbell.

Now, if the famous secret exists, then the only reason for it must be to protect family honour. I suggest, therefore, that Allan Beg is the hidden name, for what could be more abhorrent to family honour than a son standing by, while his father was hanged in his place? I believe Allan Beg was *thought* to be the murderer for the following reason. There is evidence that he and Allan Breck Stewart had gone shooting that afternoon between Lagnaha and the wood of Lettermore, and had taken the two guns from Acharn. Both of these were tied together with string and unfit for anything but sport.

When the larger gun was discovered later at Acharn, by the authorities, it was found to be still loaded with birdshot; the smaller gun had been recently fired, and the servants testified they had seen Allan Beg place it in the barn on the night of the murder. A powder horn was also found in Allan Breck's discarded clothes after he had fled.

To admit to having a gun in contravention of the Disarming Act, and to using it in the wood on the afternoon of the murder, and to admit lending Allan Breck his clothes, would also have put a rope around Allan Beg's neck, but would not have saved his father. Thus he remained in silent turmoil and his family and servants probably thought he had a hand in the murder despite his denial. That, I believe, is the origin of the famous secret although the murderer could not have been either Allan Beg or Allan Breck. The fact is, no one in Appin knew the murderer, for he was not from those parts.

However, there is every indication that many people in Appin expected Glenure would be murdered that day, but that it would happen in Lochaber. All the likely suspects made sure they were known to be in Appin and had perfect alibis. Allan Breck arranged his by calling on the Ballachulish ferryman at 12.30 pm and asking, "Has Glenure crossed over yet?" when the crossing was in full view.

But unknown to all, an assassin and his decoy were already lying in wait in the Wood of Lettermore. Such a killer would require to have certain qualifications to fit the known evidence; no compunction about shooting an unarmed man in the back; a well-maintained gun of Spanish design capable of holding a double charge; a sufficient hatred of the Stewarts to care nothing for the consequences; and lastly, a motive for the murder. There was such a man. He was Robert Oig MacGregor, youngest son of the infamous Rob Roy.

In an article (in *The Scots Magazine*, August, 1976), I told how James Mor, Rob Roy's notorious eldest son, hatched a plot to abduct the heiress Jean Key from her home near Balfron and forcibly marry her to the penniless Robert Oig. The girl was eventually released, but both James and Robert were accused of hamesucken which carried the death penalty. They escaped and were declared outlaws.

Robert Oig was also wanted for the murder of John MacLaren in Balquhidder whom he had shot in the back with his father's Spanish gun. MacLaren had been given the lease of the farm of Invernenty by the Stewarts of Appin who owned the land, but the MacGregors thought it was rightfully theirs. The Stewarts of Appin had even offered a reward of £50 for Robert Oig's capture, and the Stewarts and MacGregors had maintained a deadly hatred from that time on.

After being outlawed on 18th May 1751, both James and Robert disappeared from the Highlands. Then, in November of that year, James Mor was captured in Lochaber and brought south to the Tolbooth Jail in Edinburgh. His presence in Cameron country is very strange, but even stranger is the secret letter written by General Churchill, Commander-in-Chief in Scotland, to Lord Newcastle in London. He wrote, "James Mor is taken up on the abduction charge (Jean Key) .... we must put him in fear of his life to make him useful to us." Then follows an incredible proposal on how to free this notorious outlaw. "The greatest difficulty is to bring about his liberation without arousing suspicion of the cause."

We may indeed wonder why the capture of a dubious character like James Mor should arouse such interest that even the Government in London had to be informed. It is also known that James was carrying a military indemnity pass issued by General Churchill six years before. Strange indeed for an ardent Jacobite and outlaw.

When James Stewart of the Glen arrived in Edinburgh on 8th April 1752, after his mysterious protracted journey supposedly on behalf of the evicted tenants, he is known to have visited James Mor in prison. He had never before had any dealings with him, and it must be assumed James Mor asked him to call. The reason for this becomes clear after James Stewart's arrest. James Mor then made a statement saying Stewart had proposed to him in prison that he, James Stewart, should be given a letter to Robert Oig telling him to murder Colin Campbell. James Stewart would furnish a gun, and as reward, the Stewarts of Appin would allow the MacGregors to re-occupy the disputed farm in Balquhidder.

The prosecution suggested James Mor should be freed to give this evidence at James Stewart's trial, but the legal authorities in London refused because "the Lord Justices are induced to believe James Drummond (MacGregor) may possibly be connected with the Appin Murder". However, James Mor was cited as a witness, but wasn't called although his statement was circulated amongst the jury contrary to all the rules of justice.

It is my belief that James Mor was certainly involved in the Appin Murder, and that a deep-laid plot was afoot. Put in fear of his life, James had revealed to General Churchill the Cameron plan to murder Colin Campbell. It is even possible that Robert Oig had been hired as the gunman. Churchill took no action to prevent the murder but directed, I suggest, that it should take place in Appin, not Lochaber. For reasons of State policy, it had to be on the Ardsheal estate.

It is likely that Churchill arranged James Stewart's curious visit to the imprisoned James Mor, a man he had never met before, in order that James Mor could give a false testimony about the alleged conversation. In return, James Mor would escape with his life, and Robert Oig would receive a sum of money. It is highly coincidental that James Mor did make a miraculous escape from the supposedly impregnable Edinburgh Castle where he was held latterly, just eight days after James Stewart was hanged. He slipped across to France where he acted as a Hanoverian spy, tried to obtain a public pardon by capturing Allan Breck, but died in poverty at Dunkirk in 1754.

It seems likely that General Churchill either did not try to prevent the assassination of Colin Campbell, or he may indeed have instructed James Mor to tell Robert Oig to do it, in order to be able to arrest James Stewart and hang *him* for the murder. He was the leader of the Appin Stewarts, and to try him for treason for his part in the new Jacobit Plot would have been the spark that would have sent the Highlands up in flames. To try him for murder on the other hand, was to give him a dishonourable death. This helps to explain the extraordinary appearance of the Master of Lovat, a pardoned Jacobite and chief of Clan Fraser, as one of the prosecuting counsel at James Stewart's trial. Obviously even a pardoned Jacobite would not assist in a treason trial, but any honourable man would help to convict a base murderer! It also allowed troops to pour into Appin without arousing suspicion.

On 6th June 1752, just three weeks after Colin Campbell's murder, two men were discovered roasting a stolen sheep near the House of Glins, near Kippen in Stirlingshire. One was captured and taken to Stirling, and as the *Edinburgh Courant* reported, "It is supposed the murderer of Glenure is one of this desperate band". The prisoner gave his name as Allan Cameron, but refused to identify his companion except to say he had joined him in Lochaber in the spring. When the High Court arrived in Stirling in August, this Allan Cameron did a very strange thing. In order to avoid a trial, he petitioned to be banished for life to the American plantations. This was promptly accepted by the court. It is sinister that the circuit judges who accepted this unusual plea were those who would try James Stewart just one month later.

It seems likely this whole affair had been pre-arranged. The judges had been told to find James Stewart guilty at all costs, and so it was necessary that one of the real murderers had to avoid cross-examination at a trial. Indeed, the Stirling magistrates applied to try him on another minor charge, but the authorities in Edinburgh refused. They were adamant he was to be sent out of the country immediately. I would identify him as Allan Cameron, a cadet of the House of Callart. It is more than likely he was the decoy, the man in the brown coat and knee breeches that Mungo Campbell saw running up the hill.

It is also highly coincidental that Glins was part of the estate of the deceased Jean Key, and well-known to Robert Oig. It is also not far from the house of Auchentroig, owned by John

MacLachlan, of a sept of Clan Cameron.

A strange, suspicious character initially suspected of the murder was Red Ewan MacColl, the only man in Appin to possess a dun coat and knee breeches. It is highly coincidental that he returned to Appin from Auchentroig just two days before the murder. Had he been arranging a safe house, and did he give his clothing to Allan Cameron as a disguise?

In the precognitions, his wife stated she did not see his dun suit on the day of the murder although he wore it on the day before and the day after. At the time of the murder he was three miles away, but he arrived at James Stewart's house late in the evening. His route was perfect to retrieve his clothing.

His brother Hugh was the only person in Appin to possess a long-barrelled Spanish gun similar to that carried by the man on the hill. Many years later, such a gun was found in a tree in a glen near the murder spot. Tradition claims it as "the Black Gun of Misfortune", but it is likely it had been lent to Allan Cameron, the decoy on the hill, and never retrieved. It can be seen today in the West Highland Museum, Fort William.

The MacColl brothers' deliberate lies in court helped to send James Stewart to the gallows. Their motive for assisting in the murder plot was their hatred of Colin Campbell of Glenure who had prosecuted them for stealing cattle. Their reward was money.

Then there is a letter dated 5th May 1753, from John Campbell of Achallader: "We hear from Balquhidder that Robin Oig is returned in good plight to that country, well-mounted". Where did the impoverished Robert obtain this new-found wealth? Robert Oig was later captured at a fair at Gartmore, still carrying his father's Spanish gun with which he had shot John MacLaren in the back, and which, I suggest, he used in similar fashion to murder Colin Campbell of Glenure.

James Stewart of the Glen was hanged on a knoll at Ballachulish on a stormy day on 8th November 1752, ostensibly for a murder he did not commit, but in reality for his treasonable activities. After the removal of the leader of the Stewarts, the authorities then arrested John Cameron of Fassiefern on spurious charges. He had not been out in the Forty-Five, but was the leader of the Camerons.

There were now no leaders of the Jacobite clans in the West Highlands, and in a desperate move, the gentle Dr Archibald Cameron, brother of the exiled Lochiel, had to be sent over from France to make contact. His presence was betrayed by James Mor, and he was arrested beside Loch Katrine at the house of Brenachoil belonging to Stewart of Glenbuckie in Balquhidder.

Dr Cameron was given no trial, nor was the reason for his return ever mentioned. He was sentenced to be hanged, drawn and quartered on London's Tower Hill. His death, eight years after Culloden, and that of James Stewart, created consternation in the Highlands, but achieved the desired ends. The shocked Highlands remained quiet and the new Jacobite Uprising collapsed.

Robert Oig was hanged for the abduction of Jean Key in the Grassmarket, Edinburgh, in February 1754. He made no mention of his involvement in the Appin Murder, for, still under the influence of his notorious elder brother, he said he hoped his death would allow his brother to be pardoned.

There was an old man who died in Balquhidder in recent years. Whenever the Appin Murder was mentioned, he would close the conversation with the words, "But justice was done in the end".

I believe it was.

Neil Munro's Inveraray
by Rennie McOwan

The literary pilgrimage is a type of holiday that is becoming increasingly popular and which so far features mainly Burns and Sir Walter Scott. Attractive booklets are produced by the Scottish Tourist Board and the reader can tour the historic sites associated with the lives and writings of these two men.

It is enjoyable, too, to follow your own taste. It would be entirely appropriate to read Neil Gunn when on holiday in Caithness, or J M Barrie when in his birthplace of Kirriemuir. The pleasure of a visit to the Mearns would be deepened through reading Lewis Grassic Gibbon's *A Scots Quair*, and some might be tempted to read Thomas Carlyle before or after a visit to his restored birthplace at Ecclefechan.

A writer with a special claim for such a leisure-link is author Neil Munro. Like Sir Compton Mackenzie, he tends at the moment to be remembered for his light-hearted and humorous writing rather than for his major and serious contribution to Scottish literature. He is remembered for his Para Handy stories, written originally under the pseudonym of Hugh Foulis and featuring the Skipper himself, engineer Macphail, their capricious vessel the *Vital Spark* and high jinks up and down the west coast.

These stories provided the basic idea for the film "The Maggie" and the television series, "The Vital Spark", both of which were watched and enjoyed by hundreds of thousands who do not know or who have forgotten such books as *The New Road, John Splendid, Gilian the Dreamer, The Lost Pibroch* and *Doom Castle*.

It is true that both *The New Road* and *Doom Castle* have been televised, but the truly deep and absorbing pleasure in Neil Munro's writings is to be found by reading and re-reading his books and by spending a holiday or series of weekends in

Inveraray visiting some of the sites he brought into his books.

The old town of John Splendid's time has now gone, of course, and in its place is the so-called new burgh with its white houses, charming pends, outside stairs and discreet shops.

The third Duke and 12th Earl of Argyll decided in 1744 to move the old town to a new site known as Gallows Farland Point on the shores of Loch Fyne, at the mouth of the River Aray, well away from his own dwelling. Over the years it has developed its own character and flavour.

Inveraray, old and new, is well-known as the Clan Campbell capital and it was in the hey-day of the clans that Neil Munro set his two best-known Inveraray-centred historical novels, *John Splendid* and *The New Road*.

He was born in one of these burgh houses of character, Crombie's Land, in 1864 and attended the old parochial school and later the school in Glen Aray. The ruins of the latter can be seen to the right of the Oban road as you leave Inveraray, although it is fast disappearing under forestry. The school was set up by the Society for the Propagation of Christian Knowledge about 1870 and remained open until 1937. Munro studied Gaelic here.

One of his fellow pupils was James Chalmers, the martyr-missionary of New Guinea. Both attended a famous Sunday School, run by the Rev Gilbert Meikle in the United Presbyterian Church, built in 1836. The two boys were among a band of children some of whom walked four or five miles to the church.

Munro spent his holidays at Ladyfield Farm in Glen Aray and roamed the glens of Aray, Shira and Fyne that push north from the burgh like the prongs of a trident, glens whose uppermost ends marked a line of Campbell defence.

He explored the hills and the corries, the woods and the glens. He listened attentively to his mother's tales of the area. He swam in the burns and dozed in the heather and gradually and overwhelmingly the whole feel, sense and beauty of "shire Argile", as it was known, became a part of his boyhood being and shaped him as an adult.

Neil Munro had the perceptive mind of a good journalist, a sensitive nature and a keen interest in history. He was also a Gael to the core with a total understanding of the Highland character, although he worked successfully in an English-speaking and Lowland environment and was at home there, too.

After his first job in the office of a local lawyer, he moved to Glasgow, where he worked as a cashier in an ironmonger's shop and then joined the *Glasgow News* as a reporter. This was the move that sent him along the literary trail that was to make him famous.

In appearance, he was six feet tall with twinkling blue eyes and wavy hair. By nature, he was considerate, modest and good-humoured.

His first book, a collection of sheiling stories, was published in 1896 under the title *The Lost Pibroch*. It received immediate acclaim and is rightly regarded as a classic.

Two years later, *John Splendid* followed, a swashbuckling, yet delicate account of 17th century love and war, an outstanding historical novel .... and a must for a Munro literary pilgrimage.

Neil Munro dedicated it to his son Hugh who was killed during the First World War. You can see Hugh's name on the striking war memorial of a Highland soldier on the loch shore in the centre of the burgh. Munro was so affected by grief that he could not attend the Remembrance Day ceremony and his sorrow produced some poignant poetry.

Among his other books, *Gilian the Dreamer*, a study of boyhood days and abortive romance in the period following the Napoleonic Wars, is thought to be partly autobiographical. His last was *The New Road*. It deals with clan tensions, murder, power-seeking and love set against the background of the construction of General Wade's roads and the beginning of the end of the Highland way of life. John Buchan called it "the best historical novel since Sir Walter".

Munro's books have been criticised, of course. Despite his training as a journalist in Greenock and Falkirk, and his later eminence as editor of the *Glasgow Evening News*, he never wrote a serious, analytical, contemporary novel of the Highland scene.

His women are said to be wooden, though some would deny that. The picture of MacGregor-born Janet in *The New Road*, whose nature was "like a day on the high wild moors in spring" and her voice "like the April burns", and whose spirit was such that she went galloping north after her kidnapped lover, Aeneas MacMaster, is anything but stilted. The portrait of Gilian's spinster aunt, Mary, in *Gilian the Dreamer*, looking after her crusty brothers and daily seeing people and sights which remind her of her lost youth, is movingly drawn.

Above all, Munro was a realist. He wrote romances of the days of tartan and plaid, broadsword and targe, of heroic deeds and dark plots, but he knew human nature and its shortcomings and, above all, he could write with marvellous accuracy of the beauties of the Highland scene and could present the Highland mind and character to wider audiences.

Read (or re-read) *John Splendid, The New Road* and *Gilian the Dreamer* and head for Inveraray. For good measure, you can add *Fancy Farm* and *The Daft Days*. Divide your plans into burgh and landward, as the antique division has it. Concentrate on the burgh first, but never think of yourself in a provincial or cultural backwater.

"A small field to till, it may be said, but I know better. This parish, though you may not think it, is a miniature of the world", said Neil Munro when he became a Freeman of the Royal Burgh in 1909.

Most tourists enter by the so-called Glasgow road, over the Rest-and-Be-Thankful and down to the head of Loch Fyne-side and into the Campbell kingdom. As you curve round the head of the loch you pass the mouth of Glen Fyne, round past the mouth of Glen Shira (a delight for another day) and down to Inveraray.

Keep a sharp look-out through the trees on your left and you will see the strong tower of Dundarave Castle, ancient power-base of the Clan MacNaughton and used by Neil Munro as Doom Castle in the novel of that name. It was the book he regarded as his best, a story of the ruin of the Lamonts, of Argyll's scheming chamberlain, of the French count and the lovely Olivia. The castle, now a guest house, is a charming example of a 16th-century Scottish tower house. It was restored by Sir Robet Lorimer in 1911-12.

But it is initially Inveraray itself that concerns us and as you drive over a hump-backed bridge of handsome design you are following in the footsteps of many of the characters of the novels. This is the so-called New Bridge, built 200 years ago after floods swept away the old military bridge, and whose designer, Robert Mylne, was the architect of the new burgh.

If you are reasonably fit, make a point of going up the hill of Dunchuach, the cup-shaped hill-fort (Dun na Cuaiche), which dominates Inveraray. It is topped by a folly of a watch tower designed by Roger Morris and William Adam and erected in 1749. Behind it lies a slightly higher hill, Dun Corr-bhile, and Neil Munro wrote a moving poem in which he thanks his mother for being born in such an area and in which he mentions both hills.

He used the tower in *John Splendid,* when he depicted it as a fort. It was there the remnants of the Campbell defenders retreated as Montrose's men sacked the town. John MacIver of Barbreck (John Splendid), his friend Colin of Elrigmore, and young MacLachlan sneaked their way in and took part in the desperate battle against MacColla's Irish and the MacDonalds and Stewarts. It was from there, too, that they sallied forth to hunt for Colin's sweetheart, Betty, who had sought sanctuary in the woods of Strongara.

Across the dip between the two hills is where the author describes the attack on the fort. The defenders were unaware that it was only a feint. The real assault came unexpectedly from behind and the defenders were warned just in time by Master Alexander Gordon, the Marquis's chaplain, who, on his way to the fort, saw what was happening and at the risk of his life ran to tell them. A stirring scene of great excitement.

Neil Munro had a great love of Dunchuach. It overlooks the burgh and is a most splendid viewpoint of the woods, hills, moors and lochs of that corner of Argyll.

Wait for the sun and you will be copying John Splendid and Elrigmore who, on their return from Inverlochy, wanted their first view of Loch Fyne to be a joyful one. They stood on a knoll and saw Dunchuach rising over everything. The sun shines, the landscape glows and John Splendid launches into a paean of praise about Dunchuach. The hill is reputed to be a haunt of fairies (there is a Fairies' Knowe across the loch) and Neil Munro portrays Elrigmore musing on the mysterious people and fervently arguing for their existence.

In the burgh itself, the white Arches, a stone facade facing the Cross Green, are a famous feature. They were built as part of the new town, but Neil Munro moved them to the period of *John Splendid* when he described Montrose's men pelting under the Arches and falling on the Campbell rearguard, demoralised and leaderless after their chief had escaped by boat.

The mediaeval Mercat Cross is also featured in the novels as is Ferry Land, the ferryman's house until 1962 when the ferry to St Catherine's ceased. Neil Munro portrays Colin of Elrigmore, John Splendid and another friend, Tearlach, playing cards in the Ferry Land until late in the night when they hear the noise of feet on the road outside, "many feet and wary with men's voices in a whisper caught at the teeth — a sound at that hour, full of menace."

Munro was probably drawing on personal knowledge because as a lawyer's clerk with a growing interest in history, he would have read of the trial of the MacNicolls in 1692. Drawing on this incident, he depicts how they tried to snatch Lachlan MacLachlan, the chief's son, in a blood-feud, failed to do so during market day and crept back into the burgh at night. They broke into the home of Provost Brown, where young MacLachlan was staying the night, but on their way out with him, the roused and angry Inveraray townspeople fell on them with cudgels and sticks in a brawl that all seemed to enjoy. MacLachlan escaped, and the MacNicolls were later brought to book.

The renowned church, too, figured in *John Splendid* when Neil Munro wrote of the attempts of Master Gordon, the Marquis's chaplain, to discipline the clansmen and women into more decorous behaviour and also in *Gilian the Dreamer* as the focal point for worship and post-church gossip.

The church itself is famous in its own right and was designed in 1793 by Robert Mylne and built around 1800. The English-speaking congregation worshipped in the northern half and the Gaelic congregation in the southern half. The Gaelic end is now the church hall. The architect and the fifth Duke quarrelled about the final part, the portico on either side of the building, and it was never built.

Down by the shore is a sea-wall called the Ramparts which bounds the prison yard. Munro portrays the imaginative and almost fey Gilian going on to a ledge where the vertical wall slopes to the loch and sitting there with a book of adventure, hearing the tides roaring and letting his imagination run riot. It was a hidey-hole, safe from the ridicule of his school companions. The author was drawing on personal experience because he had sat there. It was one of his favourite spots.

He brought so much of the stones and mortar of the burgh into his books, including the scenes of the old prison in *The Brave Days*. His own house was just outside the jail wall.

When you pass down Main Street East you will see on the door of No 6 a handsome brass knocker, beautifully polished and shining.

The owners get many a knock on the door from tourists, Americans mostly, who've read *The Daft Days*, which features Lennox, a wee American girl, who comes to stay locally.

The book mentions a house with a brass hand for a knocker. Neil Munro knew it well for he and his family spent their summer holidays there with their pet dog Footles (Footles, too, features in the book).

In the back garden there is a memorial stone over Footle's grave. The inscription on the stone reads: "In memory of my dear and faithful friend Footles, who died August, 1900 in his seventeenth year."

Also in Main Street can be seen a large house entitled "MacIntyre's Highland Warehouse". It was built by Provost James Campbell between 1773 and 1780 and here, in real life, lived three veterans of the Napoleonic Wars.

One was Lieutenant-Colonel Colin Campbell who commanded the Royal Scots at Waterloo. He died here in 1833 and the names of his battles from the Peninsular War are engraved on his stone at Kilmalieu. His brother, Major General Dugald Campbell, commanded the 46th Regiment of Foot and died here in 1824. A third brother, Captain John Campbell, was Paymaster of the 48th Foot, and he died in 1859.

All three are featured in *Gilian the Dreamer*, as half-pay retired soldiers, getting on in years and living on the memories of past glories, with the exception of the Paymaster, who never saw action and who was nicknamed "Captain Mars — who never saw wars!" They were buried at Kilmalieu cemetery, about a mile from the town on the Glasgow road. It is a pilgrimage must, and before you go, take a look at the former plumber's shop at the corner of Main Street, facing the George Hotel. It was owned by the Maitland family, and Charles Maitland was a chum of Neil Munro.

On holiday from Glasgow, Neil Munro was daily to be found seated on a lavatory pedestal just inside the shop door, chatting with Peter and Charlie Maitland. Many a gem for the Para Handy stories came from these chats.

Author George Blake wrote: "Neil Munro's dearest friends, the friends of his boyhood — two of them helped to carry him to his grave in Kilmalieu — were a shopkeeper, an innkeeper and a plumber, and he was absolutely without any sense that his vocation might be regarded as finer and more dignified than theirs."

Visit Kilmalieu at evening when the light is starting to fade, with the water lapping on the shore, the birds singing, with mergansers and eiders on the loch, and you will be seeing it as Neil Munro wrote of it. It dates back to the Middle Ages and is worth exploring. Like all cemeteries it is a place of sadness and peace.

Neil Munro's gravestone is somewhat obscured now — but walk around the cemetery. It is grass-covered and tree-shrouded and has an atmosphere of great antiquity. In this place are buried many of the characters he brought into his novels. You can see the memorial stone to General Turner with a burning heart on the pillar stone; he died in Sierra Leone in 1826 and his name appears as Cape Turner on the map of West

Africa. He figures in *Gilian the Dreamer.*

There are others, including Provost Brown, who was born in 1603 and died in 1711. It is said he played a game of shinty on his 100th birthday. Neil Munro portrayed him as the father of Elrigmore's sweetheart Betty, whose house was broken into by the MacNicolls.

From the Argyll Estates woodlands walks on Dunchuach a white doocot can be seen at Carloonan farm. It was built in 1748. It is a remarkable structure and it is not surprising that it caught the Munro imagination.

It dominates much of the sombre mystery of *The New Road* and was where Aeneas MacMaster's father, Paul, was foully murdered by Argyll's factor, Duncanson, to prevent Paul discovering his treachery and double-dealing.

Duncanson could not bear to see the doocot and had a cloth hung across his window. Ninian MacGregor Campbell, the Duke's Messenger-at-Arms, and Aeneas's friend, finally unravelled the mystery of Duncanson's intrigue with the scheming Lord Lovat, the cunning trade in obsolete and useless guns shipped in by the Jacobite clans and virtuously sold to the government for good-conduct money while the real stuff was hidden in the thatch.

The doocot is one of the best-known sites in Neil Munro's writings. Remember how Ninian teased at a tangled hank of string as a kind of aid to his thought-processes: all the strands began and ended in the doocot.

Go, too, to the well of Bealach an Fhuarain, a grotto designed by William Adam and erected in 1749. You take the Oban road out of Inveraray, and just past the police station and before a bend, a ride goes left into the woods of Creag Dubh, so beloved of the author. A short distance along, a path goes off-right through the trees.

A few minutes' walking is all that's required to reach this beautiful spot. Here Colin of Elrigmore loved to come as an old man and muse on the days of youth. It was where Betty Brown, the Provost's daughter, promised to marry him and the book ends with John Splendid riding out of Inveraray to the foreign wars as a mercenary once again and with just a hint that he might, after all, be the object of her true affections. It is a place of bird-song, quiet, whispering trees and old memories.

Colin's house of Elrigmore is not on the map, but it is near Elrigbeg which is. There's not much to see nowadays, but the site is about a quarter of a mile from Elrigbeg. Glen Shira is packed with interest. Here is the Dubh Loch where the MacNaughtons had their original castle and which they abandoned for Loch Fyne-side in the 1580s when the plague came.

Here, too, is the 18th century Garadh Crom, or crooked dyke, which runs along the east side of the glen, descends to the river, crosses to Glen Aray and comes down to Loch Fyne at French Farland. It enclosed much of the Duke's ground and must be one of the longest such walls in Scotland.

There are many other interesting aspects, not directly associated with Munro's books, such as the Parson of Kilmalieu's strange prophecy of death and destruction for those who lived within the Crooked Dyke, and a witch whose cursing bone is now in the Royal Museum of Scotland and many another ancient tale.

There are so many places that struck a chord in his open heart: the Pass of Aora, The Creags, Maam and Kilblaan, Allt an Aluinn, Eilean an Eagail, Stuchgoy, Accurrach Hill, the wood of Tarradubh, High Balantyre, Ardno Hill, the Braes of Cladich, all the lovely woods, burns, pools and hills of his boyhood world which he peopled with characters and events that one would swear were alive and true.

The hills and glens of Argyll burned themselves into his soul. He has Gilian saying, "The wind in the winter trees, the gossip of the rivers, the trail of clouds, waves washing the shore at night — all these things have a tremendous importance to me".

He spoke of corries in Argyll "that whisper silken to the wind" and which had an almost magical quality about them, casting a spell upon the wanderer.

"We are the children of the hills and of the mists: the hills make no change, the mists are always coming back and the deer is in the corrie yet."

It is not enough to explore the burgh; to know Neil Munro and shire Argyle you have to spend much time on foot, or lazing, but the rewards are great. Travel by the Oban road through Glen Aray where there is a cairn-tower to his memory, sited on a hill called Creag Dubh, just outside the Argyll Estates boundary. It looks towards the former township of Carnus, the home of his forbears, and towards Loch Awe and Ben Cruachan.

The monument was unveiled in 1935 five years after his death in 1930 aged 67, and R B Cunninghame Graham, Don Roberto himself, gave the address of praise. It is worth noting that as well as the great and famous there were many so-called ordinary folk whom he considered to be the salt of the earth.

Neil Munro never quite succeeded Walter Scott and Robert Louis Stevenson as a great Scottish writer. Some of his language and his style are dating. But in his own way he was a genius. He wrote historical novels and his characters were never cardboard figures. He wrote romantically, but never hid faults or wrongdoings. He linked the world and thought-processes of the Gael of the past to an English-speaking audience rapidly losing touch with that past. He wrote at a period when people had time and inclination to read. He had a marvellous feel for Highland beauty.

He did not write enough and that, perhaps, is why his reputation waned. But happily, there are now signs of revived interest. If you don't know him, pleasure awaits you. Read and explore.

Dr Laughlan MacLean Watt said at the memorial service in Glasgow Cathedral: "As long as men love beauty and humanity the wind will keep the dust from settling on his grave." Amen to that.